NO AR

T5-AQQ-442

YA#
347   Lindop, Edmund
LIN   Great Britain and
1999   the United States

14 DAY LOAN

GREAT BRITAIN
AND THE
UNITED STATES

GREAT BRITAIN
AND THE
UNITED STATES

RIVALS AND PARTNERS

EDMUND LINDOP

TWENTY-FIRST CENTURY BOOKS
BROOKFIELD, CONNECTICUT

For John Hungerford,
my close friend since high school days,
and his lovely wife, Lura

Published by Twenty-First Century Books
A Division of The Millbrook Press, Inc.
2 Old New Milford Road
Brookfield, Connecticut 06804

Library of Congress Cataloging–in–Publication Data

Lindop, Edmund.
Great Britain and the United States: rivals and partners/by Edmund Lindop.
    p.   cm
Includes bibliographical references (p.   ) and index.
ISBN 0-7613-1471-7 (lib. bdg.)
1. United States—Foreign relations—Great Britain. 2. Great Britain—
Foreign relations—United States. Title.
E183.8.G7L56 1999
327.41073—dc21   98-12470
                                                                CIP
                                                                 AC

Jacket design by Karen Quigley
Map by Jeffrey Ward

Photographs courtesy of © The Flag Research Center: p. 12; Archive Photos: pp. 22
(Reuters/Jim Bourg), 66; North Wind Picture Archives: p. 36; UPI/Corbis-Bettmann:
p. 48; Hulton Getty/Liaison Agency: p. 84; SuperStock: p. 98 (P. J. Sharpe)

CONTENTS

GREAT BRITAIN

North Atlantic Ocean

Shetland Is.

Orkney Is.

N

0   50   100 Miles

0   100 Kilometers

Outer Hebrides

Grampian Mtns.

SCOTLAND

North Sea

Glasgow   Edinburgh

NORTHERN IRELAND

Belfast

Isle of Man

Leeds

Irish Sea

Manchester

Liverpool

Dublin

IRELAND

ENGLAND

Cambrian Mtns.

Birmingham

WALES

London

Thames River

Celtic Sea

English Channel

Atlantic Ocean

Channel Islands

FRANCE

Paris

ONE

THE ISLAND KINGDOM

Politically, Great Britain, also known as the United Kingdom, consists of four territories: England, Scotland, Wales, and most of Northern Ireland. Geographically, Great Britain is the name given to the largest island in Europe.

England, which is slightly larger than the state of New York, occupies nearly three fifths of this island. On its north, England borders Scotland, and on its west it borders Wales. Across the Irish Sea to the west lies the island of Ireland, which the United Kingdom shares with the Irish Republic.

The population of the United Kingdom is about 59 million. More than 81 percent of the people are English, and nearly 10 percent are Scottish. Much of this nation is densely settled, and 90 percent of its inhabitants live in urban areas. London, the largest city in Great Britain, has a population of more than 7 million.

Long ago, in prehistoric times, Great Britain was part of the European mainland. At the end of the last Ice Age, when temperatures rose, the huge ice caps melted, flooded the lower lands, and formed the bodies of water that surround Britain.

7

Geography provided the chief reason why Great Britain was invaded many times by wave after wave of peoples from various parts of Europe. Britain lies very close to the European mainland. At the narrowest point, the coast of southeastern England is only about 22 miles (35 kilometers) from the coast of France. These two coasts are separated by the narrow English Channel.

The first European group that invaded Britain was the Celts between 700 B.C. and 500 B.C. In the first century A.D., the Romans conquered most of the island and ruled it for nearly four hundred years. Later came the Anglo-Saxons, Danes, and Norwegians. In A.D. 1066, French Normans achieved the last successful invasion of Britain, under their leader, William the Conqueror.

AMERICA'S DEMOCRATIC HERITAGE HAD ENGLISH ORIGINS

England's democratic traditions began in 1215 when English barons forced tyrannical King John to sign the Great Charter, which in Latin was called the Magna Carta. This important document limited the king's powers and guaranteed rights to the barons.

One part of the Magna Carta said that King John must stop ordering the barons to pay him new taxes except for those that were approved "by the common council of our kingdom." These words later came to mean that the king could not require the payment of additional taxes unless they had been agreed to by the representatives of the people. American colonists later applied this principle when they objected to "taxation without representation."

The Magna Carta also declared, "No free man shall be seized or imprisoned. . . . nor shall we pass sentence on him except by the legal judgment of his peers or by the law of the land." This clause later was interpreted as meaning that all free persons had a right to trial by jury. In King John's time, however, this right did not apply to most of the English people because they were not free persons. They were serfs, bound to the land and owned by a lord. The Magna Carta, says British historian F. E. Halliday, "was a purely selfish class measure, setting forth the privileges of the aristocracy and Church, without mention of the great majority of Englishmen."[1]

As the years passed, serfdom withered and all English people became free, enabling them to gain the rights pledged to free men in 1215. But at the time when it went into effect, the most significant feature of the Magna Carta was that it bound the king to govern according to law.

The concept of a limited, representative government that provides many rights to its people—which is so important to Americans—was deeply rooted in England. In 1689 the English monarchs, King William and Queen Mary, accepted a Bill of Rights that spelled out in detail specific protections and liberties which, over a period of many years, had been secured by the English people.

Some of the Bill of Rights' provisions that limited the sovereign's power were (1) the king could not make or do away with any laws without the consent of Parliament; (2) no taxes could be raised or armies maintained except by parliamentary consent; and (3) the king could not interfere with the election of Parliament's members or with their free speech. The Bill of Rights also guaranteed the people that if they were charged with a crime, they would have a jury trial, there would be no excessive bail, and no cruel or unusual punishment would be permitted.

Americans brought from England several public offices that still function in the United States today. These include the offices of sheriff, bailiff, coroner, justice of the peace, and assessor, who evaluates property for taxation. They also adopted English units of government, such as counties, townships, and grand juries that evaluate accusations against persons charged with crimes and determine whether the evidence warrants prosecuting them in courts.

The English concept of a two-house legislature found fertile soil in America. In England the House of Lords, or upper house, consisted of appointed nobles; the members of the upper house of colonial legislatures also were appointed. Members of England's House of Commons and of the lower houses of the colonial legislatures were representatives elected by the free white men who owned property.

Thus, American colonists of English descent came to the New World with the knowledge of a political system that had been developing in England for many years. They understood that government is limited in what it can and cannot do and that each person has certain rights that the government cannot restrict or deny. And the colonists cherished the practice of electing representatives who would at least help determine their government's policies and actions.

A SHARED CULTURE

American colonists who came from England also shared the language and rich culture of their mother country. Families in Boston and London alike could enjoy the same songs and dances, art and architecture, and styles of dress.

English literature was widely read by many Americans in the colonies. The writings of philosopher-scientist Francis Bacon stressed that in order to discover truth, people had to conduct experiments and be willing to accept proven evidence that might contradict previously held ideas. John Milton and Edmund Spenser produced beautiful poetry, while Christopher Marlowe and Ben Jonson were major playwrights.

Colonists were drawn to the works of William Shakespeare, who was perhaps the greatest writer in the brilliant pageant of English literature. He had a remarkable understanding of many kinds of people and expressed the whole range of human emotions in his literary achievements. Shakespeare composed 154 sonnets, but he is best known for his plays, whose plots were based on historical and classical stories, romances, and farces. Many sayings penned by Shakespeare became part of everyday English speech.

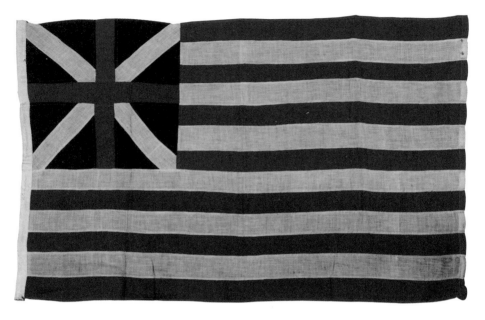

The Continental Colors was America's national flag from 1775 to 1777. It retains the British flag in the top left corner.

TWO

AMERICANS ARE FREED FROM BRITISH RULE

The first permanent English settlement on the American mainland was founded at Jamestown, Virginia, in 1607. Between then and 1733, twelve other permanent English colonies were founded along the Atlantic Coast. In addition to Virginia, they were Maryland, North and South Carolina, and Georgia in the South; Massachusetts, Connecticut, New Hampshire, and Rhode Island in New England; and the middle colonies of New York, Pennsylvania, New Jersey, and Delaware.

England did not limit its claims to the land included in these thirteen colonies. Following the discovery of Hudson Bay in 1610 by Henry Hudson, whose expedition was financed by English merchants, England claimed a large area in the northern part of North America. There it established fur-trading posts. English settlers also occupied islands in the West Indies, where rich sugar plantations were developed. By 1640, about 60,000 English men and women had moved to the New World.

Not all of the immigrants who came to the thirteen colonies along the Atlantic Coast were of English stock. The

13

Dutch established the colony of New Amsterdam in 1625, but the English conquered it in 1664 and renamed it New York. German settlers poured into Pennsylvania and Swedish settlers into New Jersey. Large numbers of Scots and Scotch-Irish immigrants moved into the foothills and valleys of the southern Appalachian Mountains. (Beginning in 1707, the Scottish people were classified as British because in that year Parliament passed an act uniting England and Scotland to create Great Britain.)

A few blacks were brought from Africa to Jamestown in 1619. As time passed and the plantation system mushroomed in the South, huge numbers of African blacks were sold as slaves to white owners. By 1763 it was estimated that African Americans accounted for about 18 percent of the total population in the British colonies.

Besides Great Britain, France and Spain also possessed large areas in North America. During the seventeenth and eighteenth centuries, Britain engaged in numerous wars with its imperial rivals. The most important conflict was the Seven Years' War (1756–1763), in which British troops, aided by colonial volunteers, soundly defeated the French.

By the Treaty of Paris in 1763, France surrendered to Great Britain all its territory on the North American continent and also French holdings in India. Britain acquired Canada and all of the land France had held east of the Mississippi River. "The successes of the Seven Years' War, which decisively defeated France in North America and India," declares British historian Paul Langford, " . . . represented a high point of imperial achievement."[1]

BRITAIN TIGHTENS ITS CONTROL OVER THE COLONIES

The British flag flew over the thirteen colonies along the Atlantic Coast for more than 165 years. During most of this long period, British rule was quite lax, and the colonial gov-

14

ernments generally were permitted to run local affairs with considerable freedom.

The British did impose a series of navigation laws to control trade in the interest of achieving prosperity throughout the empire. The Navigation Act of 1663 ordered that imports to the colonies from other European countries must pass through England and pay customs duties there and again at the colonial ports they entered. By raising the price of non-English goods, this act was intended to enlarge the colonial market for English products. But the colonists often evaded paying customs duties by smuggling products into their ports.

After the Seven Years' War, a new British attitude toward the colonies emerged. The war had been very expensive, and little of its costs had been borne by Americans. The British government decided it must tax the colonists, enforce existing laws more strictly, and reduce the colonists' rights of self-government.

In 1765 Parliament passed the Stamp Act, which was intended to raise revenues within the colonies instead of customs duties collected at ports. It required purchasing and then attaching revenue stamps to more than fifty commercial articles and legal documents.

People in England were accustomed to paying stamp taxes and could not understand why Americans would object to them. "The colonists must be the [worst] beggars in the world," one Londoner remarked, "if such inconsiderable duties appear to be intolerable burdens in their eyes."[2]

The colonists' response to the Stamp Act was swift and overwhelming. Since there were no American members in Parliament, the lament of "no taxation without representation" echoed from Boston to Atlanta. A Stamp Act Congress, with twenty-seven delegates from nine colonies, assembled in New York City in October 1765. The delegates called for a boycott of British-made products until the stamp taxes were abolished.

15

The American boycott of British goods became widespread throughout the colonies and had powerful economic repercussions. Many British merchants and shippers clamored that their businesses were being ruined by the lack of colonial customers. So, in 1766 Parliament reluctantly repealed the Stamp Act.

"Had Britain failed to repeal the Stamp Act," historian Page Smith writes, "the military phase of the American Revolution would have started in 1766, with efforts by Parliament and the Crown to enforce the act with British troops met in turn by armed resistance on the part of the colonists."[3]

Parliament then passed the Townshend Acts in 1767, which placed import duties on the colonists' purchase of glass, paper, lead, paint, and tea. But the Americans revived the practice of boycotting British goods. Sales by British merchants to American buyers plummeted, and in 1770 Parliament was persuaded to repeal all of the revenue duties except for the tax on tea.

When the ships of a British company brought their tea to New York, Philadelphia, and other Atlantic ports, angry colonists forced them to turn around without unloading their cargoes. At Boston, a violent reception greeted the tea ships. On December 16, 1773, a group of irate citizens led by Samuel Adams disguised themselves as Indians, boarded the three big ships, and threw 342 chests of tea, valued at $75,000, into the harbor.

This willful destruction of property infuriated the British government, and Parliament imposed severe punishment, which the colonists labeled the Intolerable Acts. These acts provided that (1) the port of Boston be closed until the destroyed tea was paid for; (2) the powers of local self-government in Massachusetts be drastically reduced; (3) British officials charged with violent acts against colonists would be tried in English, not American, courts; and (4) Massachusetts

16

must give free lodging and food to British troops stationed in the colony.

THE AMERICANS STRIKE BACK

Americans in the other colonies were appalled that Britain had dealt such harsh treatment to Massachusetts and especially to Boston, with its busy port closed to trade. They feared that soon their mother country might restrict their rights, too.

To coordinate action against what appeared to them to be growing British tyranny, an intercolonial congress met in Philadelphia in September 1774. Twelve of the thirteen colonies (all except Georgia) sent a total of fifty-five delegates to the meeting. The First Continental Congress passed a set of resolutions recommending total resistance to the Intolerable Acts. It also called for a complete boycott of trade with Britain.

Congress sent to King George III and Parliament a Declaration of Rights and Grievances demanding the repeal of all oppressive actions taken since 1763. Even so, the delegates expressed continued devotion to the king. Reconciliation was still the American dream. Congress commended the people of Massachusetts for resisting the Intolerable Acts, but it also urged them to remain "peaceably and firmly . . . on the defensive," steering clear of incidents "that might involve 'all America in the horrors of a civil war' before George III could respond to its pleas."4

After seven weeks of deliberations, Congress adjourned on October 26, 1774. It announced it would meet again the following May if the king had not acted favorably on its demands.

A small minority of British leaders sympathized with the colonists. William Pitt declared, "I rejoice that America has resisted." Edmund Burke proudly proclaimed that "this fierce

17

spirit of liberty is stronger in the English colonies than in any other people on earth."[5]

George III and his prime minister, Lord North, were not swayed by any arguments favoring the colonists' position. By the time the king had received their petition, he had already decided that at least the New Englanders "are in a state of rebellion," and "blows must decide whether they are to be subject to this country or independent."[6]

The first of these blows were struck during the skirmishes between British soldiers and American "minutemen" at Lexington and Concord, Massachusetts, in April 1775. This brief military encounter that produced "the shot heard round the world" had widespread repercussions. Word of the bloodshed spread throughout the colonies, and armed resistance to British rule no longer could be avoided.

The following month the Second Continental Congress convened in Philadelphia. It voted to ask the colonies for troops, military supplies, and money. Congress transformed the colonial militia groups into a continental army commanded by General George Washington, sent agents to foreign countries to try to obtain allies and loans, and issued paper money to support the war effort. Yet for more than one year the delegates—some of whom still hoped for reconciliation—failed to make the final break with their mother country.

Finally, on June 7, 1776, Richard Henry Lee of Virginia introduced in Congress a resolution calling for independence. After lengthy debate, on July 2 the delegations of twelve colonies voted in favor of Lee's resolution. (New York added its vote a week later.) The famous Declaration of Independence was adopted by the Second Continental Congress on July 4, 1776.

Americans now were officially at war with probably the world's most powerful country.

THE DIFFICULT STRUGGLE FOR INDEPENDENCE

Not all of the colonists rejoiced at the decision to fight Britain. Only a little more than a third of the Americans joined the patriot cause; another third were neutral or apathetic; nearly a third remained loyal to Britain. Many Loyalists suffered greatly because they continued their allegiance to their mother country. Patriots confiscated large land holdings and personal property of some Loyalists. Mobs sometimes terrorized them and forced them to flee; they took refuge in Canada, the West Indies, or England.

In the same month that the Declaration of Independence was adopted, an impressive British fleet began arriving off the coast of New York. Consisting of some five hundred ships and 32,000 well-trained troops, it was the largest foreign military force ever sent to America. Against this awesome number of invaders, General Washington could muster only 18,000 soldiers, mostly poorly trained militiamen who had signed up for only a few months of armed service. Some of the raw recruits, seized by panic, deserted or were easily captured.

Most of the American soldiers fought bravely and often endured the lack of enough food and warm clothing. They were paid in almost worthless paper money and did not have a sufficient supply of powerful weapons and gunpowder. But even though they won some battles, mainly at Trenton and Princeton in New Jersey and Saratoga in New York, the Americans suffered many losses because of their enemy's superior forces.

Although it was not known at the time, the patriots' victory at Saratoga in October 1777 proved to be the turning point of the war because it prompted France to enter the conflict against Great Britain. The French had been thirsting for revenge against the British ever since they had been humiliated in the Seven Years' War. When the Americans won the crucial battle at Saratoga—proving they would fight hard and long for their freedom—the French decided that if they joined forces with the patriots the British could be handed a staggering defeat.

In February 1778 the French foreign minister and Benjamin Franklin, representing the Continental Congress, signed a formal alliance. It called for France to enter the war against Britain and supply enormous military and financial aid to the patriots. In return, the Americans promised not to sign a separate peace treaty with Britain and pledged to remain France's ally in the future.

American survival depended on this help from France. Washington's ragged army was small and short of arms, but with extensive French aid the tide of war finally began turning in favor of the patriot cause. From 1778 to 1783, France provided large amounts of money and military equipment, about one half of the troops fighting the British, and most of the naval power needed to oppose Britain's strong fleet.

The climactic battle of the war occurred at Yorktown, Virginia, and ended on October 19, 1781. A British army commanded by Lord Cornwallis was besieged by American and French troops and denied an ocean escape by the French navy. As Cornwallis surrendered, his band appropriately played "The World Turn'd Upside Down." Some scattered fighting continued, but after their defeat at Yorktown the British decided that their effort to hold on to their rebellious colonists was not worth more battlefield casualties and additional expenditures from their treasury.

The American negotiators—Benjamin Franklin, John Adams, and John Jay—were eager to win the best possible terms for their new country at the 1783 peace conference. In accord with the Franco-American treaty, they had been instructed by Congress to make no agreement without the concurrence of the French government. But the American diplomats disobeyed these instructions when they learned that

France wanted the future United States to become a small French puppet state with borders extending no farther west than the Appalachian Mountains. The British suspected that their hated French rivals might be planning to restore their empire in North America, and this was one reason why they gave the Americans very generous peace terms.

Besides recognizing American independence in the peace treaty, the British agreed that the new nation would encompass a huge tract of land. The Mississippi River became its western boundary. Its northern boundary reached to Canada and the Great Lakes. In return, the Americans had to make some concessions to Britain. They promised not to hinder the British from collecting millions of dollars in debts owed by the former colonists to British merchants. And they pledged that steps would be taken to restore confiscated Loyalist property to its original owners.

After the terms were settled, the Americans signed the agreement without even consulting the French. Historian Thomas Fleming says, "This was perilously close to violating America's treaty with France and unquestionably ignored the negotiators' instructions from the Congress. While Jay and Adams exulted over this display of American independence, Ambassador Franklin had the task of soothing [Foreign Minister] Vergennes's extremely ruffled feathers. He not only managed this feat with his usual finesse, but he persuaded the irked foreign minister to agree to one last loan [to the Americans]."[7]

21

The USS *Constitution*, known as "Old Ironsides," is the oldest
commissioned warship in the world. After extensive renovations,
she set sail for the first time in 166 years in July 1997.

THREE

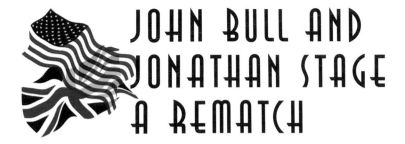

JOHN BULL AND JONATHAN STAGE A REMATCH

The British Empire, despite the loss of its thirteen American colonies, steadily increased in size. By 1815 it included Canada, Australia, New Zealand, Cape Colony in southern Africa, the subcontinent of India, the islands of Gibraltar, Malta, and Minorca in the Mediterranean Sea, and many naval bases and coaling stations in the Pacific, Atlantic, and Indian Oceans. In the years that followed, the extent of the British Empire would grow even larger.

Great Britain became the first and largest industrial giant. In 1765 James Watt, a Scottish inventor, designed a steam engine with a separate condenser that made possible the use of steam power in industry. The steam engine eventually replaced or reduced old energy sources—oxen, horses, water, and human labor. A series of remarkable British inventions for spinning thread and weaving cloth, increasingly driven by steam instead of water power, accounted for a huge growth in the number and size of mills. These flourishing mills made Britain the center of the important textile industry.

Inexpensive methods of making stronger iron were introduced. These better metals became available for many uses, including the construction of machines and later of railroad cars and tracks. Manufacturers lowered costs by grouping machines together in large factories and mills. The so-called factory system provided mass production and led to the growth of big industrial cities.

When the United States government began in 1789, with George Washington as president, the overwhelming majority of Americans were farmers. At that time, the Industrial Revolution beginning in Britain had barely touched American shores.

Many Britons regarded the United States as a weak, infant nation that probably would not survive. Sarcastically, they referred to their country as mighty John Bull and to the United States as Jonathan, its powerless, wayward son. Britain showed its disdain for the new nation by banning American ships from the lucrative trade of the West Indies and prohibiting American vessels from entering British ports unless they carried only products from their home states.

The chief reason why the British could afford to treat the United States in a degrading manner was they knew that ". . . the new republic could not survive economically without Britain. . . . The volume of Anglo-American trade actually increased after 1783 [mainly from] exports of raw cotton, which rose from an annual 15.5 million pounds in the late 1780s to 28.6 million by 1800."[1] While cotton from the American South found an ever-increasing market in English mills, Americans were purchasing large amounts of cloth made in these mills and many products manufactured in English factories.

PRO-BRITISH FEDERALISTS AND PRO-FRENCH REPUBLICANS

During George Washington's presidential administration, two distinctly different political parties emerged. Alexander Hamil-

24

ton and John Adams headed the faction that would become the Federalist party. Thomas Jefferson and James Madison were leaders of the group that soon called itself the Republican party (which should not be confused with the modern Republican party that was founded in 1854).

The Federalists believed that a powerful national government was needed to unite and stabilize the new country, guarantee law and order, and pay back the huge debt that resulted from the Revolutionary War. They argued that the national government should be directed by prosperous, educated aristocrats who had the knowledge and experience to govern wisely and unselfishly. The Federalists' support came primarily from merchants, manufacturers, bankers, and shippers engaged in foreign trade.

The Republicans opposed the Federalists' aristocratic views and insisted that the central government's power be limited and more power retained by the states. Fearful that the national government might become tyrannical, they argued that in a democratic society rule by the people was absolutely essential. Jefferson believed American prosperity would come from agriculture and envisioned a nation of small property owners who would remain fiercely independent. Farmers, artisans, craftsmen, and small shopkeepers generally favored the Republicans.

When the French Revolution began in 1789, Republicans and Federalists took opposite sides. Republicans hailed the uprising of the French people against King Louis XVI as a marvelous contagion of liberty that had spread from America to France. "All the old spirit of 1776 is rekindling," Jefferson wrote excitedly to James Monroe.[2]

Hamilton and other Federalists regarded the French Revolution as a dangerous development led by the rabble against their monarch. When the movement took a radical turn with the beheading of Louis XVI and many aristocrats, Federalists viewed this Reign of Terror with anger and disgust. And

25

when revolutionary France declared war on Great Britain in 1791, they fervently wished for a British victory.

"For Hamilton," writes historian Richard J. Barnet, "economics and blood dictated an everlasting tie with England. . . . After all, as he put it, 'We think in English.' Most important, he considered British capital and British technology indispensable to the growth of industrial capitalism in America. To the merchants and shippers on the eastern seaboard it made perfect sense to cultivate ties with Britain."[3]

Republicans, on the other hand, cheered France for attacking "hateful Britain." They recalled the tremendous amount of aid that France had given to help Americans win their independence. And they remembered the Alliance of 1778, which pledged Americans to support France in future wars.

At this critical time, President Washington turned to his Cabinet for advice regarding whether the pact with France should still be considered binding. Secretary of the Treasury Hamilton argued that the treaty was no longer in force because it pertained only to defensive wars and it had been negotiated with the French monarchy and King Louis XVI—both of whom were dead. Although partial to France, Secretary of State Jefferson conceded that a war against Britain was not in the best interests of the infant republic.

In April 1793 Washington issued a Proclamation of Neutrality declaring that the conduct of the United States toward the warring countries was to be "friendly and impartial." Whether the treaty with France was binding was not as important as avoiding war.

JAY'S TREATY

During the war between France and Britain, Americans claimed the right of a neutral nation to carry nonmilitary goods to both belligerents. France lifted some restrictions it

26

had regulating trade with its West Indian islands, and American ships began sailing to these islands to take advantage of this new opportunity.

Britain, however, refused to recognize the neutral right of the United States to trade with France or any of its possessions. In December 1793, without warning, British vessels began seizing American ships trading with the French West Indies. Within a short time, there were about 250 U.S. merchant vessels held in British ports in the Caribbean Sea. Congressman James Madison arose in the House of Representatives and angrily attacked Britain's action. Most of his countrymen agreed that the seizure of American ships was outrageous.

Another aggravating grievance was Britain's insistence on keeping forts and trading posts in the Old Northwest (the region north of the Ohio River and east of the Mississippi River). By the terms of the 1783 treaty that ended the Revolutionary War, the British had promised to hand over these forts and posts to the United States. Instead, they kept these outposts to reap rich profits from the fur trade and to slow American settlement in this region. Often they armed the Indians in the Old Northwest and urged them to be hostile to the American pioneers.

The British Navy paid sailors low wages. At various ports some of these seamen deserted their ships and joined American crews for higher pay. This practice led the British to board American ships and impress (seize) sailors. Sometimes the captured victims were British deserters, but often they were Americans who then were forced to sail under the British flag. The impressment of innocent sailors inflamed the American public.

War with Britain appeared very near. Congress gave President Washington the power to summon 80,000 state militia if necessary. In New York City, citizens began building fortifications against a possible British invasion. At Marblehead, Massachusetts, 3,000 volunteers, reviving the spirit of the minutemen, grabbed their rifles and began drilling in preparation for war.

Realizing that the military forces of the United States were pitifully weak when compared with those of Britain, Washington believed that a conflict must be prevented if at all possible. So the president sent a special envoy to London to try to negotiate a treaty that would reduce tensions between the two countries. The envoy who embarked on this important mission was John Jay, Chief Justice of the U.S. Supreme Court.

After months of discussion, Jay and Lord Grenville, Britain's foreign minister, signed what was called Jay's Treaty on November 19, 1794. The British agreed to give up their forts and trading posts in the Old Northwest—but not until June 1, 1796, and only if the United States permitted the continuation of the British fur trade with the Indians in that region. The British promised compensation for the American ships that had been seized in the Caribbean Sea—provided the United States compensated British merchants for pre-Revolutionary War debts whose collection had been impeded by state governments.

The treaty called for reciprocal trading rights between Britain and the United States but restricted American trade with the British West Indies to vessels that weighed no more than 70 tons. Moreover, these ships were banned from carrying sugar, molasses, cotton, coffee, and cacao to any part of the world except Britain and its empire.

Jay was unable to convince Grenville that the British must end their practice of impressing sailors. Nor did Grenville agree that his country would stop seizing neutral ships. Instead, he demanded that the United States give up its claim to neutral shipping rights for the duration of Britain's war with France.

The treaty that Jay brought home was so disappointing to American interests that Washington waited three months before calling the Senate into a special session to act on it. The president, however, threw his powerful support behind the pact, believing it was the only alternative to war. On June 24, 1795, the Senate barely approved the treaty by a 20 to 10 vote (a two-thirds vote is necessary for ratification), but only after striking out the clause restricting American trade with the British West Indies.

Public response to the Jay Treaty was overwhelmingly negative and spurred fierce demonstrations of anger. Anti-Jay mobs threatened Vice President John Adams' home in Philadelphia, stoned the windows of the British minister's office, and pelted Alexander Hamilton with rocks when he spoke in defense of the treaty in New York. At mass meetings from Boston to Savannah, huge crowds denounced the treaty, and some of the protesters burned Jay in effigy. Even the previously popular Washington was called the "stepfather of his country," and the most rabid treaty foes demanded that he be impeached.[4]

Despite its shortcomings, the Jay Treaty accomplished a significant objective: It postponed war with Great Britain for nearly two decades—until the United States had grown stronger and was in a better position to defend itself.

WHY THE UNITED STATES FOUGHT BRITAIN AGAIN

Britain and France quit fighting in 1802, but the following year hostilities began anew. Under the rule of Napoleon Bonaparte, France gained control of much of the European continent by 1805. Britain, with its large, powerful navy, controlled the seas. Each nation needed to cut off the imports going to the other, but the United States wanted to profit by trading with both belligerents.

Napoleon issued stern decrees that closed the European ports under his control to all British products and ordered that neutral ships which stopped at British ports or permitted searches by British naval vessels would be confiscated.

29

The British government countered with a series of Orders in Council that forbade neutral ships to trade with countries ruled by Napoleon unless they stopped first at British ports and submitted to a search for war weapons and any products from French colonies.

American ships risked seizure by either of the belligerents if they violated their rules. Between 1804 and 1807, the British seized at least a thousand American vessels and the French about half that number. Even so, American trade with these warring nations prospered; if only one ship in three escaped confiscation, a handsome profit was earned.

Still short of sailors for their navy, the British stepped up the practice of impressment. This issue took a critical turn when the *Leopard*, a British warship, stopped a United States ship, the *Chesapeake*, a few miles off the Virginia coast. The British commander demanded the right to search for alleged deserters, and when the American captain refused to comply, the *Leopard* fired three broadsides at the *Chesapeake*. Three Americans were killed and eighteen were wounded. Four sailors were removed from the U.S. ship before it proceeded with difficulty back to port.

The American public was infuriated by this humiliating episode, and President Thomas Jefferson demanded reparations and warned British warships to stay out of American waters. After the *Chesapeake* affair, Jefferson coaxed Congress to pass the Embargo Act in 1807. This radical measure prohibited all foreign trade. Jefferson figured that Britain and France would be so handicapped by the failure to receive any American goods that one or both countries would end their restrictions against neutrals trading with their enemy.

The Embargo Act backfired. It injured the United States much more than it hurt the belligerents. Thousands of sailors and dockworkers lost their jobs. Huge amounts of cotton, wheat, and tobacco piled up in warehouses. American shippers, centered in New England, spoke out strongly against the act and encouraged smugglers to violate it. As the economy appeared headed into a major depression, Congress repealed the failed Embargo Act in 1809.

Congress then passed an act permitting trade with other countries but still forbidding it with Britain and France. This partial embargo also was unsuccessful. The failure to secure neutral trading rights, along with the impressment of American sailors, were two important reasons why the United States waged war against Great Britain.

Another cause for warfare was promoted by congressmen from the West and the South known as "War Hawks." They blamed the British in Canada for arming the Indians and encouraging them to resist American settlers who were moving into the Western wilderness. The War Hawks believed that subduing the British in Canada would stop the source of Indian incitement. They also felt that Canada itself could be taken merely by marching into it, and that Florida, then owned by Britain's weak ally, Spain, could be easily seized.

When President James Madison asked Congress to declare war on Great Britain in June 1812, both houses of the legislature were deeply divided. The measure passed in the Senate by a vote of 19 to 13, and in the House of Representatives by a margin of 79 to 49. Many legislators from the shipping and commercial centers of New England and the middle Atlantic states—eager to preserve their rich trade with Britain—voted against going to war with the nation that had helped provide their prosperity.

THE WAR OF 1812

John Bull was determined to gain revenge against little Jonathan for losing the American Revolution. In 1812 the British government felt confident that it had the power to conquer the United States. It had a large, efficient army, while the Americans had only a small regular army and had to depend heavily on poorly disciplined militiamen who often refused to fight outside the borders of their own states. On the seas, the British had a tremendous advantage: their navy numbered more than eight hundred ships, and when hostilities began the entire United States Navy consisted of only sixteen fighting vessels.

Americans started the war in 1812 by attempting to fulfill their boast that Canada could be easily taken. Three separate U.S. forces drove into Canada, where they met strong resistance—which included many Loyalists who had fled there during the Revolution. All three campaigns were unsuccessful. Two of the invasions failed after the New York state militia refused to follow the regular army across the Canadian border.

In 1813 American prospects improved. Commodore Oliver Hazard Perry built a small fleet on Lake Erie that cleared the lake of enemy ships. An army of Kentucky riflemen commanded by General William Henry Harrison moved into Canada and defeated the British in the Battle of the Thames. But after winning some of the land in the present province of Ontario, the volunteers who made up most of Harrison's army returned to their homes, and the territory was abandoned.

After Napoleon was defeated and forced into exile in 1814, the British were able to send many more redcoats to America. They mounted three strong invasions against different parts of the United States. From Montreal an army of more than three thousand soldiers marched southward into New York. The invaders needed to bring their weapons and supplies over the Lake Champlain waterway, but they were defeated by an American fleet commanded by Captain Thomas Macdonough and then retreated to Montreal.

The second British expedition was more successful. About four thousand redcoats landed at Chesapeake Bay and moved inland to Washington, D.C., where five thousand American

32

militia were stationed to defend the city. But the frightened Americans panicked and ran away after ten of their comrades had been killed.

The British then burned the Capitol, the White House, and most of the other public buildings. They claimed they were retaliating for the burning of public buildings by American troops who had raided York, Canada, in 1813. Next the British ships shelled Baltimore, but they were forced to withdraw after fierce resistance from the forts guarding this Maryland city.

The third and final British expedition, aimed at New Orleans, was launched in December 1814 and ended the following January. About eight thousand redcoats, transported across the Gulf of Mexico, reached the outskirts of New Orleans. There they found waiting for them a slightly smaller force under the command of Andrew Jackson. The wily Jackson had placed his men behind barricades made of cotton bales and other materials. Foolishly, the British stayed in tight formation and waged a frontal assault. The motley American army—consisting of some regular troops, many militiamen, sailors on leave, and even a few pirates—mowed down the enemy with rifles and artillery.

In their failed attempt to seize New Orleans, the British suffered more than two thousand casualties, while American losses were limited to about seventy men. This was the most overwhelming American victory in the war. Ironically, the triumph at New Orleans occurred two weeks after the peace treaty was signed at Ghent, Belgium, but oceanic communications were so slow that word of the armistice did not reach the United States in time to prevent the needless loss of lives.

The greatly outnumbered American navy was no match for the giant British fleet. Yet in single ship-to-ship encounters American vessels achieved some stunning results. Also, in addition to regular navy ships, about 500 American privateers went to sea. (Privateers are privately owned ships

33

commissioned to fight against enemy vessels and ports.) These small but swift privateers captured or destroyed about 1,350 British cargo carriers, some within sight of the English coast. But, beginning in 1813, the full force of the Royal Navy was felt when British warships laid a tight blockade on the entire Atlantic coast. This dealt a serious blow to American foreign trade.

The Treaty of Ghent, signed on Christmas Eve in 1814, said nothing about neutral trading rights or impressment, but these issues were less important after Britain and France quit fighting. No territorial changes occurred as a result of the treaty, but provisions were made for the appointment of commissioners to meet later and settle questions of boundaries, a trade agreement, fisheries, and rights on the Great Lakes.

The United States neither won nor lost the War of 1812, which, in the parlance of sporting events, might be described as a draw. Still, Americans had reason to rejoice. Little Jonathan had held his own against powerful John Bull. Moreover, a rising spirit of nationalism was sweeping across the country. Americans now could turn their attention from warfare to concentration on territorial expansion and the development of large-scale manufacturing.

"OLD IRONSIDES": MISTRESS OF THE SEAS

In 1794 President George Washington convinced Congress to lay the foundation of the infant United States navy by appropriating money to construct six frigates. They were to be built of sturdy Georgia live oak. More than two hundred years later much of that durable wood is still soundly in place on the U.S.S. *Constitution*, one of the frigates.

The *Constitution* first slid into the sea in 1797. It was originally used to protect American cargo ships on trading missions to Europe and North Africa from the attacks of the Barbary pirates.

34

Measuring 204 feet (62 meters), the *Constitution* became the U.S. Navy's most successful fighting ship in the War of 1812. In ship-to-ship engagements from its launching until 1815, its record was forty-two victories and not a single defeat.

The *Constitution* met the British warship *Guerrière* on August 12, 1812. In the ensuing battle, which lasted about a half hour, the *Constitution* fired more than 950 rounds into the enemy ship and then set the ruined hulk on fire. When a British cannonball bounced harmlessly off the side of the American frigate, a sailor exclaimed, "Huzzah! Her sides are made of iron!" This gave birth to the ship's famous nickname.

"Old Ironsides," now moored in Boston Harbor, is the world's oldest commissioned warship still afloat. She has undergone extensive renovations from time to time. On July 21, 1997, to celebrate the 200th anniversary of her commissioning, this national treasure was cheered by large crowds on the docks as she set sail for a one-hour voyage.

35

Covered wagons, such as those shown here at Scotts Bluff, Nebraska, were the main form of transportation along the Oregon Trail. The trail was a major route to the West in the 1840s. Both Britain and the United States claimed Oregon at that time.

FOUR

GREAT BRITAIN AND U.S. EXPANSION

Between 1803 and 1848, the United States acquired a large part of the North American continent. In 1803 it purchased from France the huge Louisiana territory, which doubled the size of the country. Following the War of 1812, an increasing number of Americans—freed of European quarrels for the first time in their history—pushed westward.

Ironically, to help set the stage for its expansion, the United States made two agreements with its former enemy, Great Britain. To prevent a threatened naval armaments race on the Great Lakes, the two nations signed the Rush-Bagot Pact in 1817. It provided for demilitarizing the Great Lakes by removing from them all warships except a few small vessels needed to prevent smuggling. "This accord," declares British historian Birdsall S. Viault, "led to an enduring peace between the United States and Canada."[1]

The second pact was the Convention of 1818. It opened the waters near Newfoundland and Labrador to fishers from the United States. More important, it established the 49th parallel as the northern boundary of the Louisiana Purchase land all the way from the Lake of the Woods in Minnesota to the

37

Rocky Mountains. This made it possible for the United States to acquire territory that later became most of the present states of North Dakota, Montana, and Idaho. Another provision of the Convention of 1818 called for "joint occupation" of the disputed Oregon territory for the next ten years. This meant that for at least another decade Oregon would remain "free and open" to both American and British fur traders and settlers.

BRITAIN AND THE MONROE DOCTRINE

In the early 1820s, Russia threatened the territorial expansion and commercial shipping of the United States in the Northwest. The Russians had established trading posts and some forts stretching from the coast of Alaska southward almost as far as San Francisco Bay. In 1821 Czar Alexander I declared that Russia owned all the land north of the 51st parallel, which includes much of present-day British Columbia, and he warned that no foreign ships would be permitted to sail within 100 miles (161 kilometers) of this land.

Besides the trouble posed by Russia in North America, the United States also was concerned about recent developments in other parts of the Western Hemisphere. Between 1804 and 1823, most of Spain's colonies in South America and Central America, along with Mexico, had revolted and established independent governments. Both Great Britain and the United States made lucrative trading arrangements with these young Latin American nations.

The monarchs of France, Austria, Russia, and Prussia adamantly opposed new countries anywhere in the world and were enraged when the Latin Americans won their freedom from Spain. Rumors spread that one or more of these European powers intended to help Spain regain its lost colonies. When these rumors reached London and Washington, D.C., British and American government leaders were determined to stop all efforts to quell the Latin American republics.

In August 1823 George Canning, the British foreign minister, contacted Richard Rush, the American minister stationed in London. Canning proposed that the two nations issue a joint declaration stating they strongly opposed the acquisition of former Spanish colonies by any European power and promising that Britain and the United States would take no more territory in Latin America for themselves.

Rush sent Canning's proposal to President James Monroe, who then sought the advice of former presidents Thomas Jefferson and James Madison. They both felt that a joint declaration with Britain might protect the interests of the United States with little risk, since the mighty British Navy would be expected to guard the Latin American states from intervention by any foreign countries. President Monroe seemed inclined to accept this advice until he learned that his secretary of state, John Quincy Adams, opposed the arrangement.

For three reasons, Adams believed that a joint declaration with Britain would not serve the best interests of the United States. First, he doubted that the European powers would carry out their threat to help Spain regain its lost colonies, and he felt that Russia would scale back its demands for a large part of the Pacific Northwest. (Russia soon did agree to reduce the southern boundary of its Alaska territory from the 51 degrees [51st parallel] it had claimed to 54 degrees, 40 minutes.)

Second, Adams opposed Canning's offer because he believed that joining Britain as a junior partner would result in an undignified loss of American prestige. He told President Monroe, "It would be more candid, as well as more dignified, to avow our principles explicitly to Russia and France, than to come in as a cockboat in the wake of a British man-of-war."[2]

Third, Adams was suspicious of Canning's motives regarding the section of his proposal that promised that neither the British nor the Americans would take over additional

39

lands in Latin America. Adams felt that this was a veiled attempt by the British to prevent future American efforts to gain Cuba or other areas where the Spanish flag had flown or was still flying.

President Monroe agreed with Adams, and the secretary of state's ideas were incorporated into the president's annual message to Congress presented on December 2, 1823. Included in this message were the principles that later came to be known as the Monroe Doctrine. The chief features of the doctrine were (1) the Americas no longer were open to colonization by European powers; (2) Europe was warned not to interfere with the political systems of the newly established Latin American republics or to intervene in any of the affairs of the Western Hemisphere; (3) existing European colonies in the Americas were in no danger from the United States; and (4) the United States would not intervene in purely European affairs.

The Monroe Doctrine angered European diplomats at the time it was announced, and for decades foreign nations denied that it had any legitimacy other than as a statement of American ambitions. Nevertheless, the Monroe Doctrine became one of the foundation blocks of United States foreign policy and was upheld by American statesmen in several disputes during the nineteenth and twentieth centuries.

A BRITON FUNDS AMERICA'S TREASURE CHEST

In July 1835 an official at the United States Embassy in London received a copy of a will bequeathing about half a million dollars for the creation in Washington, D.C., of "an Establishment for the increase and diffusion of knowledge among men."[3]

The benefactor was James Smithson, the wealthy, illegitimate son of a British lord, who had published papers on chemistry, mineralogy, and botany before his death in 1829.

40

No one knows for sure why Smithson made his unusual bequest. He had never been to America and did not appear to have any contacts there. Smithson may have left his fortune to the United States because he resented the British social system that barred an illegitimate son from inheriting his father's title and from holding a high position in the military or the church.

At first Congress was reluctant to accept the gift. Senator John C. Calhoun argued that it was "beneath the dignity of the United States to accept presents of this kind from anyone."[4] But in 1846 President James K. Polk signed into law the bill that gave birth to the Smithsonian Institution. Ten years later, its first building, mainly a research center, opened its doors.

Today the Smithsonian Institution is a complex of fourteen Washington museums and two in New York, five research institutes, and the National Zoo. It has about 6,700 full-time employees and 5,000 volunteers who study, restore, and care for 140 million artifacts.

One of the Smithsonian's most popular attractions is the National Air and Space Museum. Among its treasures are the Wright brothers' Kitty Hawk aircraft, the plane that carried Charles Lindbergh across the Atlantic Ocean in 1927, a *Saturn V* rocket engine, and the *Apollo 14* command module. It has a Web site: www.nasm.edu

THE WEBSTER-ASHBURTON TREATY

The border between Maine and the Canadian province of New Brunswick had not been clearly defined. Both the United States and Canada claimed thousands of square miles of fertile land near the Aroostook River.

In 1838 American settlers from Maine began clashing with lumbermen from New Brunswick. Tension heightened in February 1839 when Canadian authorities arrested American

Rufus McIntire for trying to expel Canadians from the disputed land. McIntire had acted on orders from officials in Maine.

Both New Brunswick and Maine militias massed along the frontiers of the Aroostook Valley. President Martin Van Buren was authorized by Congress to call for 50,000 soldiers in case the conflict triggered a war with Great Britain. But neither side wanted hostilities, and Van Buren sent General Winfield Scott on a peace mission to the region. Scott arranged a temporary truce that defused the crisis until the border issue could be settled.

In 1842 Britain sent diplomat Lord Ashburton to Washington, D.C., to meet with Secretary of State Daniel Webster. They drew up a treaty that was satisfactory to both sides.

It gave Canada a large portion of the disputed land, including enough to provide an important land route from the St. Lawrence River to New Brunswick. The United States received what it wanted most—much of the Aroostook Valley—and territory that slightly enlarged New York, New Hampshire, and Vermont. More important, the Webster-Ashburton Treaty provided the United States with some very valuable territory that was a long distance from Maine. This was land between Lake Superior and the Lake of the Woods, on which later were found the rich Mesabi iron deposits—a major source of the ore needed for the nation's iron and steel industries.

The 1842 Webster-Ashburton Treaty ended the U.S.–Canadian boundary disputes east of the Rocky Mountains and for the moment averted a possible military clash between Great Britain and the United States.

"FIFTY-FOUR FORTY OR FIGHT!"

No provision of the Webster-Ashburton Treaty determined whether Great Britain or the United States owned the land west of the Rocky Mountains that was bordered on the north by Russian Alaska and on the south by Mexican-held California. Since 1818 this vast territory—larger than France and Germany combined—had been considered "jointly occupied" by Britain and the United States.

Both countries had claims to this land known as the Oregon territory. The British insisted that Sir Francis Drake had discovered the Oregon coast in 1579 and that other Englishmen later went into that territory. James Cook and George Vancouver had stopped there in the eighteenth century, and Alexander Mackenzie had journeyed on the first overland trip to Oregon in 1793. The extensive fur-trading activities of the Hudson's Bay Company and its domination of Oregon for many years further buttressed British claims.

American claims to the region also were substantial. New England traders had sailed to the Oregon coast to buy furs from the Indians in the late eighteenth century. Captain Robert Gray had discovered the mouth of the Columbia River in 1792, and the Lewis and Clark expedition (1804–1806) had pushed into Oregon and claimed that land for the United States. John Jacob Astor's Pacific Fur Company was active in the region and founded Astoria on the Columbia River in 1811.

Despite their conflicting claims, for many years the Americans and the British did not show much interest in the remote Oregon territory. The region was governed loosely by the Hudson's Bay Company, which gathered furs over a large part of the Pacific Northwest and established some farms and ranches. Before the mid-1830s, the few Americans in Oregon were on trading and trapping expeditions.

In 1833 a religious magazine reported that the Indians in Oregon wanted to learn about Christianity; this aroused the enthusiasm of several churches. The Methodists sent a minister, Jason Lee, to start a mission in the Willamette Valley in 1834. Two years later the Presbyterians sent Marcus Whit-

43

man and his wife, Narcissa, to found a mission near present-day Walla Walla, which is now in the state of Washington but was then part of the Oregon territory. And Father Pierre Jean de Smet, a Catholic priest, worked among the Indians on the western slopes of the Rockies. The missionaries sent letters back home that praised the fertile soil of the Oregon country.

As word spread that this region could yield rich crops and valuable timber, more and more people east of the Rockies began to catch "Oregon fever." In 1842 the first substantial group of settlers traveled in covered wagons to the Pacific Northwest. The journey along the Oregon Trail, which began at Independence, Missouri, and ended at the Willamette Valley, was long and difficult. But the stalwart pioneers were willing to endure hardships in their quest for free, arable land that offered the possibility of a more prosperous life.

By the mid-1840s, at least five thousand Americans had reached Oregon by this overland route. They had set up their own temporary government and began demanding that the Oregon territory be annexed to the United States. The pressure of the American settlers steadily mounted, and it became apparent that the decision as to which country would control Oregon could not be delayed much longer.

Several attempts were made to break the deadlock over Oregon. Britain had repeatedly offered to compromise by conceding to the United States that part of Oregon which lay south of the Columbia River, including the fertile Willamette Valley, where most of the Americans had settled. Three times the United States had proposed to compromise by drawing the border at the 49th parallel, thus accepting Britain's claim to the area north of that line. The only region still in dispute was the area between the Columbia River and the 49th parallel (which includes most of the present state of Washington).

The controversy over Oregon might have been settled quickly and quietly if the Democratic party had not made it an emotional issue in the presidential campaign of 1844. The Democrats nominated James K. Polk, an ardent expansionist, for the presidency. He was eager to add to the Union both Oregon and Texas, which had won its freedom from Mexico in 1836. The platform of the Democratic party pledged "that our title to the whole of the Territory of Oregon is clear and unquestionable; that no portion of the same ought to be ceded to England or any other power. . . ."[5] Claiming all of Oregon up to the southern boundary of Alaska (54 degrees, 40 minutes) gave the Democrats a couple of exciting slogans: "Fifty-four Forty or Fight!" and "All of Oregon or None!"

Polk won the election and in his inaugural address repeated that Americans had "clear and unquestionable title" to the whole Oregon territory. Furthermore, he asserted that "the United States government would protect the American emigrants to Oregon with laws and 'the benefits of our republican institutions,' looking toward annexation in the near future."[6]

The British government was offended by Polk's blustering, overbearing attitude. "When questions arose in Parliament, the prime minister, Sir Robert Peel, declared that Britain also had clear and unquestionable rights in Oregon."[7] The British press was even more strident. The influential *London Times* proclaimed that "the territory of Oregon will never be wrested from the British Crown, to which it belongs, but by WAR."[8]

Neither country, however, wanted to resort to military action to settle the Oregon question. Britain at that time was plagued by serious domestic problems, and its manufacturers were dependent on Americans for consuming many of their products and for providing most of the cotton needed for their mills. In May 1846 the United States had gone to war against Mexico, so President Polk was determined to dispose of the Oregon issue without risking a second conflict with Britain.

After a round of negotiations, a treaty dividing the disputed land at the 49th parallel was agreed to by both nations and ratified by the Senate in June 1846. This line on the map still constitutes the border between the state of Washington and the Canadian province of British Columbia, with one small exception—Vancouver Island, whose southern tip is slightly south of the 49th parallel, remains a part of British Columbia.

A CENTRAL AMERICAN CANAL IS OF INTEREST

Britain as early as the 1840s considered building an Atlantic-Pacific canal in either Nicaragua or Panama, which was then a province of New Granada (now Colombia). This angered government leaders in the United States, who claimed that a British canal in any part of Central America would violate the Monroe Doctrine. But the British had already acquired control over land in Nicaragua on the Atlantic coast side of a possible canal.

American interest in an interoceanic canal was sparked by the steady migration to Oregon and by the discovery of gold in California in 1848, which was attracting thousands of new settlers to the West. Suddenly there was an urgent need for faster transportation to the American Pacific coast than was provided by horses and oxen-pulled wagons traveling across the plains and mountains. So the United States secured exclusive transit rights across Panama in an 1846 treaty with New Granada.

Great Britain and the United States appeared to be on a collision course over the issue of building and operating a canal in Central America. As tension between the two countries mounted, Britain in late 1849 sent Sir Henry Bulwer, an able diplomat, to confer with Secretary of State John Clayton in Washington, D.C.

Their negotiations resulted in the Clayton-Bulwer Treaty of 1850. It provided that (1) neither country would build an interoceanic canal in Central America without the consent and cooperation of the other; (2) neither country, should it build the canal, had the right to fortify it or exercise exclusive control over the waterway; and (3) the canal would be open to ships of all nations on equal terms.

America and Great Britain were allies in World War I. The celebration shown in this photo took place in Washington, D.C., on November 11, 1918, the date of Germany's surrender.

FIVE

FROM RIVALS TO PARTNERS

The growing rift between the North and the South dominated the American political landscape in the 1850s. A series of controversial events widened the division between the two sections of the country. The Kansas-Nebraska Act of 1854 established two new territories, Kansas and Nebraska, and provided that the inhabitants of the territories should themselves decide the status of slavery (according to the doctrine of popular sovereignty). This led to savage fighting between proslavery and antislavery factions in what became known as "bleeding Kansas."

In response to the Kansas-Nebraska Act, the modern Republican party was created in 1854 and pledged to resist the extension of slavery into the territories. The Supreme Court's Dred Scott decision in 1857 forbade Congress to prohibit slavery in the territories, which was a victory for the Southern cause. Two years later abolitionist John Brown and his followers unsuccessfully attempted to seize the government arsenal at Harpers Ferry, Virginia, where they hoped to obtain the armaments needed to start a large slave uprising.

Northerners feared that permitting slavery in the territories soon to become states would add more proslavery members to Congress, and the South then would be in a strong position to defeat any antislavery legislation. Southerners also worried about upsetting the balance of power in the national government. If legislators from free states held at least two thirds of the seats in Congress, slavery could be abolished by an amendment to the Constitution.

Relations between Northerners and Southerners in Congress became so strained that in 1860 one Southern senator declared, "No two nations on earth are or ever were more distinctly separated and hostile than we are here . . . how can the thing go on?"[1]

Many Southerners began to argue that rather than giving in to Northern domination, their states should secede (withdraw) from the Union. They claimed the same right to form their own separate government that their ancestors had asserted when they declared their independence from Great Britain in 1776.

Republican Abraham Lincoln was elected president in November 1860 on a platform promising to prevent the spread of slavery into the territories. His election triggered the secession of Southern states from the Union. Before Lincoln's inauguration in March 1861, the seven states of the Deep South had seceded, and four other states followed later. In February 1861 the departing states formed the Confederate States of America.

Jefferson Davis, president of the Confederacy, authorized Southern military forces to fire on Fort Sumter, a United States fort on an island in the harbor of Charleston, South Carolina, after Union ships tried to bring supplies to the fort. This bombardment on April 12, 1861, was the opening salvo in a devastating war that lasted four years. More Americans—Northerners and Southerners—were killed or injured in the Civil War than in any other conflict in the history of the United States.

50

BRITAIN AND THE AMERICAN CIVIL WAR

British opinion about the war in America was divided, partly along class lines. Many people in the upper classes considered the Southern planters as fellow aristocrats and applauded the Confederacy's determination to exist as an independent nation. Moreover, the low-tariff policies of the South were more favorable to British traders than the high-tariff policies adopted by the North.

The lower classes and the social reformers in Britain, who were engaged in a crusade to achieve more democratic conditions in their own country, rejoiced at the prospect of the American slaves winning their freedom, since Britain had already abolished slavery. They were disappointed, however, when President Lincoln at first believed that the restoration of the Union was a more urgent goal than the emancipation of the slaves. In his inaugural address, Lincoln stated that he had no intention ". . . to interfere with the institution of slavery in the States where it exists."

Southerners were eager to have powerful Britain as their ally in the war. To accomplish this, they stressed the importance of cotton to the British economy. Eighty percent of cotton used in Britain's textile industry, which employed four million workers, came from the Southern states. The textile mills provided one third of all British exports. To create pressure on London, the South held back cotton exports in 1861, but this strategy failed to make Britain its ally.

Neither public opinion nor economic considerations dictated British government policies. War against the United States was a dangerous course of action and could have disastrous consequences if Union armies invaded and conquered Canada. Southerners hoped that Britain would recognize the independence of the Confederacy, but the prime minister and Parliament feared that this might provoke the North to take military revenge. Unless and until future battles indicated that the Union would lose the war, the British government would go no further than declaring its neutrality and recognizing the "belligerent rights" of the Confederacy.

President Lincoln proclaimed a blockade of the South in April 1861. At that time the U.S. Navy had available only three warships to intercept vessels before they reached any of nearly two hundred ports along a coastline of 3,500 miles (5,600 kilometers). By the end of 1861, about 150 ships were on the blockade patrol, and most of the South's major ports were at least partially closed. But hundreds of small blockade-runners continued to slip past the Union ships.

The blockade was bound to cause friction between Britain and the United States, but historian Bradford Perkins says Britain knew that "to challenge the blockade might lead to war."[2] Moreover, the British realized that, as the world's greatest seapower, in the future they would probably use the weapon of blockade against some potential enemy. So they did not deny the authority of the Union to impose a blockade. Nor did the British strongly object when U.S. ships intercepted neutral vessels en route to a neutral port and searched them for contraband. After all, this was an act that the British had repeatedly committed against United States ships during their war against Napoleon.

A serious incident involving neutral rights occurred in November 1861. An American warship commanded by Captain Charles Wilkes stopped a British mail steamer off the coast of Cuba. Wilkes seized James M. Mason and John Slidell, two Confederate diplomats, who, having slipped through the blockade, were traveling to England. The British ship then was allowed to continue its voyage, but Mason and Slidell were imprisoned in the United States.

Americans rejoiced because the capture of these two men was similar to the impressment that the British had practiced against U.S. sailors before the War of 1812. Captain Wilkes became an instant hero in the North and was awarded a gold medal by Congress.

The British people were incensed by this kidnapping of diplomats and correctly claimed it was a violation of international law. Britain's foreign minister demanded the release of Mason and Slidell, along with an apology from the United States government. Troop reinforcements were sent to Canada, and plans were initiated for sending a fleet of British warships across the Atlantic Ocean.

President Lincoln and Secretary of State William Seward found themselves in a difficult position. They did not want to condemn Wilkes's action, which was popular with Northerners, but, more important, they could not risk war with Britain at a time when all their military forces were needed to combat the Confederacy.

Seward first convinced himself and then the president that the seizure of Mason and Slidell violated the long-standing American doctrine supporting neutral rights and freedom of the seas. Lincoln then had the men released and allowed them to resume their voyage to England. Seward sent Britain an explanation of Wilkes's action (not an apology), and the British concluded that this was a satisfactory, if surly, response to their demands.

Another serious crisis, this time initiated in London, threatened in 1862. The Southerners had recently won an impressive series of victories, but the casualties on both sides had been heavy. Britain, probably with the aid of France, considered mediating the Civil War and bringing an end to the rampant slaughter on American battlefields. The prime minister and the foreign minister agreed "that the time is come for offering mediation to the United States Government, with a view to the recognition of the independence of the Confederates."[3]

Britain's mediation attempt would have led to two separate countries, the United States and the Confederacy. Since this proposal would have quashed the North's goal of restoring the Union, it was met with strong resistance by Lincoln and his advisers. Secretary of State Seward informed London that Europe could commit no graver error than to become involved in the American war.

Before the mediation plan was put into action, two events occurred that caused its demise. In September 1862 General Robert E. Lee led his Southern army into western Maryland as a first step toward an invasion of Pennsylvania. He hoped this campaign would demonstrate that the Confederacy was going to win the war and that the North therefore should stop fighting. But the South's advance was dramatically halted by Northern troops in the battle of Antietam, and the forecast of the Confederacy winning the war was suddenly dimmed.

In the same month, President Lincoln issued a preliminary Emancipation Proclamation that freed all slaves in areas controlled by the Confederacy. (The proclamation would go into effect on January 1, 1863.) Now that the South was retreating on the battlefield and the North was fighting a crusade against slavery instead of simply trying to restore the Union, no more was heard of British attempts at mediation.

Anglo-American relations faced still another crisis in 1862–1863, when the Confederacy contracted with a British company, Laird Brothers, to build several warships. Lincoln's minister to Britain, Charles Francis Adams, protested vigorously, but the *Alabama* and *Florida* left the British shipyards and began spectacular careers as Confederate commerce raiders. Before it was finally sunk by a Northern warship, the *Alabama* captured or destroyed fifty-eight ships, while the *Florida* seized or destroyed an additional thirty-eight Union vessels.

An even greater danger appeared when Laird began constructing for the Confederacy ironclad rams capable of breaking the North's blockade by piercing the hulls of wooden ships. Adams angrily wrote Lord Russell, the British foreign minister, "It is superfluous [beyond what is required] in me to point out to your Lordship that this is war."[4] Aware that permitting these armored rams to leave England might provoke

54

hostilities with the United States, the British government had already decided to buy the ships for its own navy.

Following the Civil War, the United States government pressed claims against Great Britain for damage done to Northern ships by the *Alabama* and other British-built Confederate raiders. The matter was resolved after the Treaty of Washington (1871) provided for the submission of disputes between Britain and the United States to an international tribunal. In 1872 that tribunal decided that Britain had failed to use "due diligence" to prevent the Confederate raiders from crossing the Atlantic Ocean to prey on Northern ships. It awarded $15,500,000 to the United States, thus bringing to an end the stormy episode in which the American Civil War had almost spread into a much larger conflict.

JUMBO: THE CAUSE OF AN INTERNATIONAL FUROR

In 1865 the African elephant Jumbo was purchased by the London Zoological Gardens. When he was fully grown, Jumbo stood 12 feet (3.7 meters) in height and weighed 7 tons (6,500 kilograms). He was the largest creature in captivity. During his seventeen years at the zoo, Jumbo carried on his back thousands of youngsters, including the children in Queen Victoria's family.

P. T. Barnum, the famous American showman, purchased Jumbo for his circus in 1882. The English public was indignant at the sale and showered Barnum with a storm of protests. The editor of the *Daily Telegraph* cabled Barnum that "all British children distressed at Elephant's departure; hundreds of correspondents beg us to inquire on what terms you will kindly return Jumbo."[5] United States minister James Russell Lowell remarked at a banquet in London that "the only burning question between England and America is Jumbo."[6]

Jumbo's name became associated with anything huge. London restaurant owners honored the giant elephant by featuring on their menus Jumbo soup, salad, stew, and pie. Store-keepers sold Jumbo cigars, fans, ties, and overcoats.

Barnum thrived on the publicity given to his animal celebrity, but he refused to break his contract for the sale of Jumbo. For four years the famous elephant helped make Barnum's "Greatest Show on Earth" popular throughout the United States, and performances sold out daily.

On a foggy night in 1885, Jumbo's trainer was leading him down railroad tracks when the elephant was struck from behind by a speeding train. The collision derailed two locomotive cars and killed both Jumbo and the train's engineer. Barnum arranged for Jumbo's skeleton to be restored and given to the American Museum of Natural History in New York City, where it can still be seen.

BRITISH DIPLOMAT MEDDLES IN A PRESIDENTIAL ELECTION

In the presidential election of 1888, Democrat Grover Cleveland was running for reelection against Republican Benjamin Harrison. Since most Irish Americans hated Great Britain, the Republicans attempted to win their votes by charging that Cleveland was subservient to the British.

George Osgoodby, a sly Republican in California, sent a letter to Sir Lionel Sackville-West, the British minister in Washington, asking for advice about how to vote, and he signed it "Charles F. Murchison." Osgoodby pretended he was an American citizen of English descent and wanted to vote for the presidential candidate who most favored British interests.

Sackville-West fell into the trap that Osgoodby had set for him. He replied that the Democratic party seemed to want to promote friendly relations with Great Britain and that he preferred Cleveland to Harrison.

Osgoodby quickly turned the British minister's letter over

to Republican headquarters, which released it to the press. As expected, the letter's publication in numerous newspapers stirred the wrath of many anti-British voters of Irish descent. Cleveland was incensed that a British diplomat had interfered in an American election and demanded that the British government recall him as its minister to the United States.

The close election resulted in Cleveland winning the popular vote by only about 91,000 votes. Harrison, however, won the electoral vote, 233 to 168, and thus the presidency. Harrison carried most of the states with large Irish-American populations, including New York, Massachusetts, and Pennsylvania.

In 1892 Cleveland and Harrison competed in a rematch. Cleveland was victorious, thus becoming the only president to win two terms in the White House that were not consecutive. Grover Cleveland was the nation's twenty-second and twenty-fourth president and the only Democrat to win the presidency between 1860 and 1912.

QUARRELS FOLLOWED BY IMPROVING RELATIONS

For many years the Samoan Islands in the South Pacific Ocean had been used as stopping places for whaling vessels and trading ships. In 1878 the United States negotiated a treaty with the Polynesian chiefs promising them protection in return for receiving a lease on the splendid harbor of Pago Pago on Tutuila Island. Germany and Great Britain obtained similar treaties the following year, giving them naval station rights in the Samoan Islands.

Competition among these three countries caused escalating strife. In 1889 the crews of three German, three American, and one British warships were preparing for possible hostilities. Suddenly, a huge hurricane destroyed all of these ships except the British vessel. This calamity was followed by a temporary solution: The Samoan Islands would be gov-

57

erned by a three-way protectorate operated by the Americans, Germans, and British.

Ten years later, there was another quarrel over control of the Samoan Islands. This time, however, Britain was not involved, since that country had become fully occupied by its Boer War in South Africa. The United States and Germany then divided the islands between themselves, with the Americans continuing to hold Pago Pago.

A more important disagreement occurred over land in South America. For many years Britain had claimed disputed territory lying between Venezuela and its colony of British Guiana. The Venezuelans had repeatedly urged arbitration, but the prospect of an easy solution declined when gold was discovered in the disputed area.

In 1895 President Grover Cleveland demanded that the British government agree to arbitration that would determine the correct boundary between Venezuela and British Guiana. When Lord Salisbury, the British prime minister, ignored his message, Cleveland ordered his secretary of state, Richard Olney, to send Britain a strongly worded complaint. Olney then informed Salisbury that the United States was now supreme in the Western Hemisphere and that by taking more land in South America the British would be violating the Monroe Doctrine. After a delay of four months, Salisbury finally replied that the Monroe Doctrine had no standing in international law and was not relevant to the boundary controversy.

Cleveland then sent an urgent note to Congress, requesting an appropriation of $100,000 to appoint a commission that would draw the boundary line in the disputed area without consulting Britain. He implied that if Britain would not accept this boundary, the United States would fight for it. The British ambassador in Washington, D.C., declared that Cleveland's belligerence had produced in Congress and the American public a condition that could only be described as hysterical.

For a short time, war seemed imminent. The British fleet

was alerted, and in the United States talk about seizing Canada was revived.

Fortunately, cautious second thoughts prevailed. Britain was then concerned about the rising military might of Germany—especially the German fleet that was challenging British naval supremacy—and also about imperialist rivalries with France and Germany in Africa. The British had no desire to fight the United States over a boundary in a remote South American jungle.

Just the thought of such a conflict led to a flood of petitions in England opposing military action. One petition, with several thousand signatures, said: "All English-speaking peoples united by race, language and religion, should regard war as the one absolutely intolerable mode of settling the domestic differences of the Anglo-American family."[7]

Salisbury finally agreed to arbitration, and the British were awarded most of the disputed territory. The British prime minister's willingness to permit arbitration helped lay the foundation for a growing Anglo-American friendship.

This friendship was further enhanced during the Spanish-American War in 1898. Most of the countries of Europe sided with Spain and blamed the United States for fighting an imperialist war against a much weaker nation. The British press and people, however, had strong pro-American feelings. Soon after the United States declared war, thousands of red, white, and blue streamers decorated London buildings, and that year American Independence Day, July 4, was celebrated by many Britons.

A year later the British began fighting the Dutch Boers in South Africa. Although some Americans, remembering past conflicts with Britain, favored the Boers, the United States government remained officially neutral but privately sided with the British. Also, American bankers supplied loans that financed about one fifth of Britain's war costs.

Because it was preoccupied with the Boer War and Germany's expanding strength, the British government abandoned some of the projects it had considered, including a canal in Central America. In 1900 Secretary of State John Hay and Julian Pauncefote, the British ambassador to the United States, signed a treaty that would replace the 1850 Clayton-Bulwer Treaty and permit the United States alone to construct and own—but not fortify—a canal in either Panama or Nicaragua.

The Senate refused to ratify this treaty because it lacked the provision allowing the United States to defend such a canal. So a second Hay-Pauncefote Treaty granting Americans their wish to fortify the Atlantic-Pacific waterway was negotiated in 1901 and ratified by the Senate. As had happened in the Venezuela-British Guiana border dispute, once again Britain had given in to American demands.

Theodore Roosevelt recognized this historic turn in Anglo-American relations and wrote a friend, "I feel very strongly that the English-speaking peoples are now closer together than for a century and a quarter; . . . for their interests are fundamentally the same, and they are far more closely akin, not merely in blood, but in feeling and principle, than either is akin to any other people in the world."[8]

WORLD WAR I

"In 1900 Great Britain seemed supreme," according to British authors David Dimbleby and David Reynolds. "The scramble of the great powers for control of Africa had brought her Egypt, much of East Africa and a vast southern African domain carved out by Cecil Rhodes. At her Diamond Jubilee in 1897 the Queen Empress [Victoria] governed a fifth of the globe. Her subjects were equal in number to the rival empires of France, Germany and Russia combined."[9]

Nevertheless, Britain faced serious concerns as it entered the twentieth century. The industrial output of the United

States now surpassed that of its former mother country. Moreover, the largest nations in Europe were engaged in a dangerous arms race. Fearful of being caught alone in a future war, Britain and other countries frantically lined up allies.

When a widespread war began in August 1914, on one side the chief combatants were Britain, France, and Russia (together known as the Allies), and on the other side the major powers were Germany, Austria-Hungary, and Turkey (called the Central Powers). Later, Italy, Japan, and finally the United States joined the Allies.

The world had never before experienced such a devastating conflict. Millions of the men who went into battle over a period of four years were killed, and many more were severely wounded. At first this savage encounter was called the Great War, but after another catastrophic conflict started in 1939 it was renamed World War I. Historians asserted that World War I was the first "total war" involving large civilian populations and aerial bombing and marked the beginning of modern times.

After the first shells were fired, President Woodrow Wilson declared that this was not America's war and cautioned his countrymen to be "neutral in fact as well as in name." Many Americans still traced their ancestry back to British roots, and they generally favored the Allied cause. But another 8 million of the nation's 105 million people in 1914 were of German ancestry, and most of the 4.5 million Irish-Americans had little sympathy for Britain, which they felt had oppressed Ireland for many generations. Regardless of ances try, most Americans initially wanted to stay on the sidelines and observe the fighting in Europe from a safe distance.

The United States, however, was intent on exercising the rights of a neutral nation to freedom of the seas and trade with both sides. It soon became the largest shipper to the Allies and also pursued on a much smaller scale trade with the Central Powers. But Britain clamped a tight naval blockade on Germany and its allies and warned neutrals not to ship war supplies to ports held by the Central Powers. It began forcing American ships into British ports for inspection and seizing military cargoes headed for enemy nations. President Wilson charged that these actions violated neutral rights, but Britain replied that it had legitimate reasons for enforcing the blockade.

In February 1915 the Germans retaliated against the British blockade by launching a submarine ("U-boat") campaign against both armed and unarmed Allied ships. The U-boats, which struck stealthily from beneath the ocean's surface, broke long-established international rules of warfare that said unarmed ships must not be sunk without warning and only after providing safety for their passengers and crews. The Allies and the United States insisted that unrestricted submarine attacks on merchant ships and passenger liners were illegal and dastardly.

The horrors of unrestricted submarine warfare were clearly revealed in May 1915 when a German U-boat torpedoed and sank the *Lusitania*, a British liner en route from the United States to England. The death toll numbered 1,198 persons, including 128 Americans. Wilson angrily protested this attack and demanded that Germans protect noncombatants in war zones. In response Germany claimed that the *Lusitania* was carrying a large cargo of munitions to Britain, and later investigations proved this charge was true.

Blunting the German submarine campaign was vital to the Allies and to the American economy. Vast amounts of munitions, clothing, and food were being sent from the United States to the Allies. U.S. exports to the Allies nearly quadrupled from prewar levels. Britain, France, and Russia, however, were on the verge of bankruptcy because of their staggering war costs. So American bankers and investors came to their rescue and lent the Allies huge sums of money—some estimates ran as high as $10 billion.

In the two months following the sinking of the *Lusitania*, forty-seven Americans lost their lives on various Allied vessels. In March 1916 a U-boat torpedoed the French passenger liner *Sussex*, injuring several Americans. President Wilson then issued an ultimatum: "Unless the Imperial German government should now immediately declare and effect an abandonment of its present method of submarine warfare, the government of the United States can have no other choice but to sever diplomatic relations."[10]

At that time the Germans were confident they would win the war within a few months. So they promised to end the sinking of merchant and passenger ships without warning and to make provisions for safeguarding the lives of passengers and crews. This *Sussex* pledge was considered a diplomatic triumph for Wilson and helped him win reelection in 1916 by campaigning on the slogan, "He kept us out of war."

Soon after the *Sussex* pledge, German leaders began to realize that their victory was not certain. In the single battle of the Somme River in the summer and fall of 1916, German losses on this French battlefield were estimated at more than 450,000. Consequently, in January 1917 the Germans reversed their policy and resumed unrestricted submarine warfare without warnings. They realized that this about-face probably would bring the United States into the war. But the Germans gambled that the severe damages they could inflict on Allied shipping would bring their enemies to their knees before the Americans were able to send large armies to Europe.

United States merchant ships were sunk in February and March 1917. Moreover, on March 1 the United States learned that British intelligence had intercepted the Zimmermann telegram, which was sent by the German foreign minister to the German ambassador in Mexico. It said that should the United States enter the war, if Mexico allied with Germany the Germans would help it recover Texas, Arizona, and New Mexico.

No longer could President Wilson maintain neutrality. Proclaiming that "the world must be made safe for democracy," Wilson asked Congress on April 2, 1917, to declare war on Germany. Four days later, Congress granted the president's request by the large margins of 82 votes to 6 in the Senate and 373 to 50 in the House of Representatives.

When the first troops in the American Expeditionary Force, commanded by General John J. Pershing, reached France, they were a small, partially trained outfit, which the French called "doughboys." Not until October 23—more than six months after Congress had declared war—did the first detachment of American soldiers see battle action. By December, 200,000 U.S. military personnel were in Europe, and this number expanded to nearly 2 million before hostilities ended.

At the time that Americans finally began fighting in France, the Allies were in danger of defeat. Russian soldiers were completely demoralized, and in November 1917 their government was seized by V. I. Lenin and his Communists. (Lenin pulled Russia out of the war four months later.) Italian troops were experiencing reverses. Both the French and the British were suffering enormous casualties without forcing the Germans to surrender. And large numbers of French soldiers, fearing death in the trenches, had quit fighting.

The U-boats were sinking British ships at an alarming rate. But the American Navy went into action shortly after the United States declared war. It joined the British Navy in convoying U.S. troop ships and war supplies to France, and the two navies embarked on a massive campaign to destroy German submarines. By early 1918, the U-boat attacks had virtually ended.

Late in May 1918, the advancing Germans had pushed to within 40 miles (64 kilometers) of Paris. The Americans helped stem the tide at the battles of Château-Thierry and Belleau Wood. By mid-July, the Allied armies were preparing to mount a mighty counteroffensive from which the Germans would never recover. An American force numbering about 240,000 soldiers won an impressive victory in September, dislodging their enemies from the vital Saint Mihiel area.

As part of the final Allied assault, involving several million men including 1.2 million Americans, General Pershing's troops undertook the Meuse-Argonne Forest offensive. Heavy fighting lasted forty-seven days from late September to early November, with the Germans falling back farther and farther. The British, French, and Americans now were advancing on every front.

On November 11, 1918, the Germans conceded defeat and agreed to the Armistice ending hostilities. United States troops had made a substantial contribution to the Allied cause in the last six months of the war. But American assistance had come so late, while the other combatants had been fighting such a long time, that it is not correct to assume that the United States was chiefly responsible for winning the war. The Americans, with about 53,000 soldiers, sailors, and marines killed in battles and another 63,000 dead from wounds or diseases, lost fewer men in the entire war than the French and British lost in the single battle of the Somme River.

British war dead totaled 947,000, and over 2 million soldiers were wounded. France's war dead numbered 1.4 million and Germany's 1.8 million. Counting the casualties of all the countries engaged in World War I, nearly 10 million lost their lives and 20 million more were wounded.

These were staggering, almost incredible statistics. Yet scarcely two decades later, they would be eclipsed by an even more devastating war that enveloped Europe, Asia, and North Africa.

65

War again strengthened the ties between Great Britain and the United States in the 1940s during World War II. Here British Prime Minister Winston Churchill and U.S. President Franklin Roosevelt meet aboard the USS *Augusta*.

SIX

WORLD WAR II STRENGTHENS BRITISH-AMERICAN TIES

The huge British Empire became even larger after World War I. The postwar settlements extended British rule to almost a half-billion people and a fourth of the earth's land surface.

The Treaty of Versailles ending the war with Germany deprived the Germans of their colonies and assigned them as mandates to various countries that had composed the wartime Allies. The mandate system was designed to protect the native populations and prepare them for independence, but in practice the system proved to be little more than annexation by every nation awarded mandates.

German East Africa passed to Great Britain, which renamed this mandate Tanganyika. Germany's African colonies of Togoland and the Cameroons were divided between Britain and France. The British-held Union of South Africa acquired German Southwest Africa.

Under the terms of the treaty ending the war between Turkey and the Allies, Turkey lost land in the Middle East. Britain acquired Palestine and Mesopotamia (Iraq) as mandates, while Syria and Lebanon became French mandates.

67

Before World War I, Britain had given dominion status to Canada, Australia, New Zealand, and the Union of South Africa. These dominions were self-governing in their domestic affairs, but Britain continued to control their foreign policies. They all had joined loyally with Britain in World War I, but all were stirred by a nationalism of their own and a desire to achieve virtual independence.

An imperial conference in 1926 provided that the dominions were legal equally with Britain and free to conduct their own foreign policies. All were "autonomous communities within the British Empire, equal in status, in no way subordinate one to another in any aspect of their domestic or external affairs, though united by a common allegiance to the crown, and freely associated as members of the British Commonwealth of Nations."[1] This meant that no act of the British Parliament would be binding on any dominion without its approval, and that the only legal tie among the Commonwealth nations was their allegiance to the same monarch.

Significant changes in the British economy emerged after World War I. No longer was Britain the world's largest creditor, lending more money than any other nation. This role had passed to the United States. War debts owed by the Allies to the Americans totaled more than $10 billion. Of this amount, more than $4 billion was owed by Britain alone. Already saddled with the huge costs of the war, Britain had great difficulty making these debt payments.

High postwar tariffs enacted by the United States government interfered with Britain's reducing part of its debt by selling products to Americans. The British in turn also erected high tariff walls, but they showed "imperial preferences" by permitting the Commonwealth nations to pay lower tariff rates on goods shipped to the British Isles.

Britain had been the world's largest exporter before World War I, but this also changed during the 1920s. By 1929

Britain's share of world exports declined to 12 percent as the United States's share climbed to 16 percent.

ARMS REDUCTIONS AND PACIFISM

The supremacy of the British fleet—which had prevailed since the reign of Queen Elizabeth I—began to fade after World War I. In an attempt to prevent another major war, Britain and other powerful nations undertook drastic arms reductions, including the size of their navies. Moreover, in the 1920s, the British did not have the funds to take part in an expensive ship building program that would have been needed to keep pace with the expected expansion of the American and Japanese navies.

Naval disarmament was one of the chief issues acted upon at an international conference that met in Washington, D.C., in 1921–1922. The negotiators agreed that the United States, Great Britain, and Japan would scuttle some existing capital ships and not complete the construction of others. Capital ships were mainly large battleships displacing more than 10,000 tons of water.

The naval agreement resulted in the destruction or failure to complete the construction of sixty-six capital ships totaling nearly 10 million tons. The negotiators established a 5-5-3 ratio by which Japan was entitled to 60 percent of the battleships allotted to both Great Britain and the United States.

The Washington Conference Treaty did not include cruisers, destroyers, or submarines. In January 1930 another naval conference was convened in London. There the 5-5-3 ratio was extended to large cruisers and a 10-10-7 ratio was established for other categories of ships.

In the 1920s and 1930s, disarmament also was applied to armies and warplanes. The armed forces of Britain, France, and the United States were greatly reduced. The U.S. Army, which numbered in the millions at the end of World War I, was transformed in the postwar years into a puny force smaller than the army of Portugal.

Pacifism became the prevailing mood among the former Allies. Half of all French men between the ages of twenty and thirty-two had been killed in World War I. "To the French it was inconceivable that such a holocaust should be repeated. French strategy was therefore defensive, and sparing of manpower. If war came, the French expected to fight it in the elaborate fixed fortifications, called the Maginot Line, which they built on their eastern frontier facing Germany, from the Swiss [border] to the Belgian border."[2]

Many people in Britain and the United States then believed that World War I had been a tragic endeavor, that little had been gained from it, and that armament manufacturers and bankers had been the chief beneficiaries of the conflict. There was an almost paralyzing fear of another world war that very likely would be more horrible than the first one. A symbol of the opposition to war was the Oxford Oath, by which British university students, beginning in 1933, pledged that they would never take up arms for their country under any conditions. This movement soon spread to college students in the United States.

As Americans in the mid-thirties recalled the ways they had helped the Allies before entering World War I, they insisted that the United States must have laws which would prevent such practices from occurring again. So, between 1935 and 1937, Congress passed a series of strongly worded neutrality acts. These laws put a ban on the sale and transportation of munitions to all belligerents and forbade loans to any nation at war. If the fighting powers bought nonmilitary supplies, such as food and clothing, they were required to pay in advance and take the goods away in their own ships. Moreover, Americans were warned that if they traveled on the passenger ships of belligerents, they did so at their own risk.

70

GATHERING WAR CLOUDS AND AMERICA'S RESPONSE

In 1933, the same year that Franklin D. Roosevelt became president, Adolf Hitler became the Fascist dictator of Germany. Hitler and Benito Mussolini, the Fascist dictator of Italy, scorned democracy, which Mussolini described as a "rotten corpse." The Fascist rulers called for a totalitarian state in which total devotion to the government replaced the individual's rights and freedoms. Only totalitarian rule, they asserted, can bring true strength and prosperity to a nation.

Mussolini built a sizable army that invaded the African kingdom of Ethiopia in 1935 and conquered it the next year. Hitler defied the Treaty of Versailles' restrictions placed on German armaments and forged the most formidable armed forces in the world. In addition to millions of well-trained Nazi soldiers, they included many warships and tanks, and airplanes more numerous and powerful than those of any other country.

In 1936 Hitler and Mussolini formed an alliance known as the "Rome-Berlin Axis." A short time later, Japan, also ruled by a military dictatorship, joined the alliance, which was called the Anti-Comintern Pact because all three countries opposed the spread of communism.

Hitler's Nazis annexed Austria in 1938, and then Hitler threatened to seize the Sudetenland, a section of Czechoslovakia where three million Germans lived. As the war clouds increased, President Roosevelt proposed a peace conference be held under the leadership of the United States. But the British prime minister Neville Chamberlain, angry because isolationist America had steered clear of any involvement in Europe's problems, rejected the offer.

Instead, Chamberlain pursued a policy of appeasement, hoping to satisfy Hitler's demand for the Sudetenland in exchange for a promise by the Nazi dictator that he would seek no additional land. The government heads of Great Britain,

71

France, Germany, and Italy held a conference in Munich, Germany, in September 1938. There the British and French leaders decided to sacrifice the Sudetenland, without the approval of Czechoslovakia, rather than risk war. Chamberlain returned to London, clutching the signed agreement, which he said promised "peace in our time."

Hitler, however, had badly deceived Chamberlain. In March 1939 he sent his storm troopers into Czechoslovakia to take the remainder of that country. This was the signal that finally awakened Britain, France, and the United States to the likelihood that the German dictator's huge appetite for more land could not be curtailed except by war. Feverishly, the British and French rushed to rearm, but by this time Hitler had gained an enormous head start in putting together a mighty military machine.

On January 4, 1939, President Roosevelt addressed Congress and declared that the forces of aggression were growing stronger and that there must be cooperative efforts to meet this challenge. The United States, he said, must use all means "short of war" to deter the aggressors. The president then asked Congress for more than $1.3 billion to enlarge America's military forces. This amounted to 15 percent of the nation's total budget, which was an unprecedented expenditure for defense measures in peacetime.

HOT DOGS: A FOOD FIT FOR A KING

As Great Britain appeared headed for war, King George VI and his wife, Queen Elizabeth, visited the United States for four days in June 1939. He was the first reigning British monarch to set foot on the soil of the former American colonies.

About 3.5 million cheering Americans lined the streets of New York City when the royal couple's motorcade proceeded to the World's Fair at Flushing Meadows, New York. Later, the king and queen stopped at Washington, D.C., where proper protocol was carefully observed. American government officials were formally introduced to the royal guests.

Then the famous foreigners completed their American visit at President Roosevelt's ancestral Hyde Park home nestled in a beautiful wooded area near the Hudson River. Here, in a placid, rural part of New York State, they were entertained in an atmosphere of cordial informality. The king even donned a bathing suit and swam in the Roosevelt pool. At night after the others had gone to bed, he and the president stayed up to discuss the alarming developments in Europe, and Roosevelt pledged that if war broke out he would do all in his power to help Britain.

One highlight of the Hyde Park visit was an American-style lawn picnic. The genial hosts served hot dogs (the king ate two), smoked ham, strawberry shortcake, and beer. When this menu was mentioned in the press, some people claimed it was degrading and disrespectful to the royal couple. But, like most Americans, the king and queen seemed to thoroughly enjoy the picnic and its hot dogs.

THE END OF APPEASEMENT

When Hitler began clamoring for land in Poland, the British and French finally stood firm and warned him that they would use military force to resist an attack on Poland. Meanwhile, in late August, Germany and the Soviet Union signed a nonaggression pact including a secret agreement that, in the event of war between Germany and Poland, the Soviets would receive eastern Poland in return for their neutrality.

On September 1, 1939, a German blitzkrieg (lightning attack) that included troops, tanks, and warplanes struck Poland. Two days later Britain and France declared war on Germany. World War II had begun.

The United States was officially neutral, but President

Roosevelt's reaction was very different from that of Woodrow Wilson when World War I began. Roosevelt said, "I cannot ask that every American remain neutral in thought, for even a neutral cannot be asked to close his mind or conscience."[3]

In November 1939, at the president's urging, Congress revised one of the neutrality acts to permit the sale of arms to belligerents on a "cash and carry" basis. "The new law was a landmark," writes historian Akira Iriye, "indicating the end of American isolation from world conflicts."[4]

Poland was conquered within a month. During the winter of 1939–1940 there was a lull in the fighting, and this period was known as the "phony war." It ended on April 9, 1940, when the Germans overran Denmark and attacked Norway. British troops landed on the Norwegian coast, but they were forced to withdraw a few weeks later.

On May 10 the Germans launched a spectacular offensive, invading northern France, the Netherlands, Belgium, and Luxembourg. That evening Prime Minister Neville Chamberlain resigned, having lost a vote of confidence in the House of Commons. He was replaced by Winston Churchill, who became Britain's great wartime leader.

The German blitzkrieg once again proved unstoppable. When Belgium surrendered late in May, a huge Allied army was trapped at Dunkirk, a city near the French-Belgian border and close to the English Channel. The British were determined to rescue the Allied soldiers and transport them across the channel. Between May 26 and June 4, using both warships and about six hundred private craft—ranging from rowboats to yachts—the brave English people miraculously rescued from the beaches of Dunkirk about 338,000 troops, two thirds of them British.

When once-powerful France fell in June, Americans suddenly were jolted out of their isolationist complacency. It now appeared that the British Isles were in grave danger of being the next victims on Hitler's list of conquests. If this happened, the

United States later might have to fight Germany, Italy, and probably Japan without a single strong ally.

The immediate American response to the desperate situation in Europe was a hurried and vast expansion of U.S. military forces. Between June and September 1940, Congress appropriated $16 billion for defense measures, including the construction of many airplanes and warships.

Five days after Winston Churchill became prime minister, he had sent President Roosevelt an urgent request for fifty overage destroyers. After Dunkirk the British had only 68 destroyers fit for service (compared with about 450 in 1917). By July 1940, British ships were being sunk at a rate nearly four times as fast as new ships could be built. In desperate need for more destroyers, Churchill cabled on July 31: "Mr. President, with great respect I must tell you that in the long history of the world, this is a thing to do now."[5]

Roosevelt wanted to grant Churchill's request, but he knew that the American public might complain because sending ships to Britain would violate United States neutrality and could be considered a free gift to a country possibly on the verge of extinction. Churchill responded "that Great Britain would never surrender, and that even if England was subjugated, the empire, armed and guarded by the British fleet, would carry on the struggle."[6]

Using his power as commander in chief of U.S. forces, President Roosevelt bypassed Congress and made a deal with Britain in September 1940. The United States gave Britain fifty overage destroyers (some dating back to World War I) in exchange for 99-year leases on eight British sites in the Western Hemisphere, stretching from Newfoundland to British Guiana. These sites would be used for American naval and air bases.

To launch their expected invasion of Britain, the Germans first needed to gain control of the airspace over the English Channel and southern England. During the first phase of the

75

battle of Britain, in August and September 1940, the Luftwaffe (German Air Force) tried to destroy Britain's much smaller Royal Air Force (RAF) and its bases. But aided by the newly invented radar warning system, the brave RAF pilots inflicted heavy damages on the attacking planes. This action prompted Churchill's famous tribute to the RAF: "Never in the field of human conflict was so much owed by so many to so few."[7]

Unsuccessful in its attempt to win control of the air, the Luftwaffe in the autumn of 1940 began relentless bombing attacks on London and other English cities. Coventry was destroyed, and the industry of other cities was severely disrupted. Bombing raids killed thousands of people (about 14,000 in London alone), but the spirit of the courageous Britons to survive on their "tight little island" was never diminished. German air losses were so heavy that Hitler abandoned his plan to invade England.

The British, however, were hard pressed to pay for all the needed military equipment and supplies. Churchill informed Roosevelt of the dire consequences that could result if they were not obtained soon. FDR then proposed "lend-lease" to Congress: The United States would lend or lease arms and other military materials to any country whose defense was deemed vital to American security. Despite cries from isolationists that Hitler would consider the lend-lease policy positive proof that the United States had renounced its neutrality, in March 1941 the measure passed in the Senate with a two-thirds majority and in the House with an even more one-sided vote of 317 to 71.

Britain was the immediate beneficiary of the lend-lease law. In May 1941, China, which Japan had invaded in 1937, also became a recipient of lend-lease goods. After Germany invaded the Soviet Union in June 1941—which proved to be a colossal mistake—the Soviets too received vast amounts of lend-lease aid.

Although they had frequently corresponded, the first

meeting of Churchill and Roosevelt occurred secretly on shipboard off the coast of Newfoundland in August 1941. There they issued a joint declaration of war goals, even though it would be another four months before the United States officially declared war. The Atlantic Charter told the world that the war was being fought to permit self-government for all peoples, disarmament, freedom from want and fear, global economic cooperation, and some type of postwar organization to keep the peace.

Transporting lend-lease goods to Britain safely was difficult. After German submarines sank nearly half of a twenty-two-ship British convoy during one night in April 1941, FDR ordered the U.S. fleet to patrol halfway across the Atlantic Ocean and inform British ships whenever they detected German vessels. U.S. Marines in July occupied Iceland to prevent a possible German invasion of that island and to help protect ships headed for England. Two months later, when the U.S. destroyer *Greer* was attacked by a German submarine, President Roosevelt issued a "shoot on sight" order to American naval commanders in the Atlantic. After another destroyer, the *Reuben James*, was sunk in October, Congress approved arming U.S. merchant vessels.

Churchill urged Roosevelt to take the official, climactic step: Ask Congress to declare war on Germany. But FDR hesitated, waiting for some major dramatic incident that would unite the American public and Congress in wholehearted support of such a declaration. Roosevelt told Churchill privately, "Everything was being done to force an 'incident' that could lead to war."[8]

WINSTON CHURCHILL: GALLANT LEADER

The son of Lord Randolph Churchill and Jennie Jerome, an American, Winston Churchill was born at Blenheim Palace in England in 1874. He was a mediocre student and was sent to

77

military school rather than to a university. As a young man, Churchill fought in British imperial campaigns in India and the Sudan. Acting as a London newspaper reporter in the Boer War, he was captured in an ambush but had a daring escape.

At the age of twenty-six, Churchill was elected to the House of Commons in 1900. In 1911 he was appointed first lord of the Admiralty and was hailed as a brilliant young man with a promising political future. But four years later, during World War I, he resigned that position after being harshly criticized for devising an Allied naval expedition that failed to break enemy defenses at Gallipoli blocking Allied access to the Balkans and the Black Sea.

After serving briefly as a colonel in an infantry battalion in France, Churchill in 1917 was readmitted to the House of Commons and also was appointed minister of munitions. Unable to reestablish his reputation as a future national statesman, Churchill dropped out of politics in 1922. He returned to the House of Commons in 1924 but had little influence on Parliament until World War II began in 1939 and he again became first lord of the Admiralty.

When he became prime minister in the dark days of 1940, Churchill said he had nothing to offer except blood, toil, tears, and sweat. However, as the war progressed, he became a towering leader in the struggle to preserve freedom and democracy. He made significant contributions to the Allies' strategy and inspired the entire free world by his eloquent speeches and indomitable spirit (symbolized by his familiar optimistic "V for Victory" salute).

Rejected as prime minister by the British voters in 1945, Churchill continued to serve in the House of Commons and to write historical books and his memoirs. His highly praised *Second World War* helped him win the Nobel Prize for Literature in 1953. Once again he became prime minister in 1951 and held that office until his resignation, at the age of eighty, in 1955.

When Churchill died in 1965, he had undoubtedly earned a niche in the pantheon of the giants of the twentieth century.

THE UNITED STATES ENTERS WORLD WAR II

Japan, not Germany, provided the dramatic incident that brought the United States into World War II, with the bombing of Pearl Harbor on December 7, 1941. The next day the United States and Great Britain declared war on Japan, and three days later Germany and Italy declared war on the United States. Roosevelt cabled Churchill: "Today all of us are in the same boat with you and the people of the Empire, and it is a ship which will not and can not be sunk."[9]

The first major decision that confronted the United States government was how to divide its military forces. Some of Roosevelt's advisers first wanted to concentrate on fighting the Japanese, who were successfully attacking many places in the Pacific Ocean. By the spring of 1942, the Japanese had conquered the American possessions of the Philippine Islands, Guam, and Midway, the British colonies of Malaya, Singapore, and Hong Kong, and the Dutch East Indies.

President Roosevelt, however, decided that since the British and the Soviets were fighting for their survival, most of the American troops, ships, and warplanes initially would be sent to battle Germany and Italy. Until these two European powers were defeated, a much smaller operation would be waged against Japan.

The next question was where should the Americans first attack the Fascist armies. General George Marshall, chief of staff of the U.S. Army, favored an early assault across the English Channel against Nazi-held France. Joseph Stalin, the leader of the Soviet Union, whose armies were suffering heavy casualties on the Eastern front, also argued for a second front in France that would relieve his hard-pressed troops. Churchill, however, remembering the enormous Allied losses

79

in France during World War I, opposed a 1942 offensive across the channel that would be led mainly by untested U.S. soldiers. Instead, he insisted that American forces should first strike at the German and Italian armies that had occupied former French colonies in North Africa.

Lack of military preparedness for a huge invasion of Europe was one reason Churchill preferred moving against the enemies in North Africa. "But the Prime Minister's emphasis was also on the preservation of imperial greatness, especially in the eastern Mediterranean and the Middle East," observes British historian Kenneth 0. Morgan.[10]

Churchill won the argument about where the American forces first should be used, but President Roosevelt continued to be concerned about Britain's obsession to hang onto all its possessions. Even though the American president and the British prime minister became close friends, during the course of the war FDR frequently expressed his belief that parts of the British Empire, especially India, were eager to achieve their independence. Churchill, however, remained adamantly opposed to this idea. "We mean to hold our own," he declared. "I have not become the King's First Minister in order to preside over the liquidation [elimination] of the British Empire."[11]

The first large-scale American forces, commanded by General Dwight D. Eisenhower, went into action in North Africa in November 1942. They occupied Morocco and Algeria and advanced into Tunisia. Trapped between American troops moving from the west and British troops pushing forward from the east, the Germans and Italians were forced to surrender in May 1943. North Africa was now in Allied hands and could be used as a springboard for the invasion of southern Europe.

In January 1943 Roosevelt and Churchill met at Casablanca in Morocco. Churchill sought further Allied operations in the Mediterranean, including an invasion of the Balkan countries, which he called the "soft underbelly" of

Europe. He suggested that a Balkan campaign by British and American troops might restrict the postwar influence of Soviet power in Eastern Europe. Roosevelt—perhaps unfortunately—overruled the possible Balkan attack, but the two leaders agreed to demand the unconditional surrender of the Axis powers.

American and British soldiers invaded the Italian island of Sicily in June 1943 and conquered it in five weeks. Then they landed in southern Italy in September. Mussolini already had been deposed by his own people, and the new Italian government surrendered quickly. Hitler, however, had anticipated the fall of Italy, and he rushed in hordes of Nazi soldiers, who took control of about two thirds of the country.

Meanwhile, the battle of Stalingrad, which began in the fall of 1942, was the turning point on the Eastern front. On the bloodiest single battlefield of the war, the Soviets withstood a fierce siege at Stalingrad and then counterattacked. In 1943 and 1944, the Red armies were on the offensive, first driving the Nazis out of Russia and eventually back across Eastern Europe.

Late in 1943 Roosevelt and Churchill met Stalin in Tehran, Iran. The three leaders (known during World War II as the Big Three) discussed plans for the 1944 second front in France. At this meeting, Stalin pointed out that the Soviet Union had suffered many more losses in its armed forces and civilian population than the two other Allies and was entitled to extend Soviet power in Eastern Europe following the war.

For many months, German cities and military installations were subjected to heavy American and British bombing raids as a prologue to opening the second front in Western Europe. Finally, the long-awaited and carefully planned invasion of France was launched on June 6, 1944 (D day). In the largest amphibious operation in history, involving about 4,600 ships and thousands of airplanes, American troops landed on Omaha and Utah beaches in Normandy, while

British and Canadian soldiers assaulted the nearby Gold, Juno, and Sword beaches. General Eisenhower served as Supreme Allied Commander, and his deputy was British Air Chief Marshall Sir Arthur Tedder.

People throughout the free world anxiously waited to learn whether the Allies would gain footholds on the beaches of Normandy or be driven back into the ocean. The fighting was savage and the casualties were heavy on both sides, but the Allies' beachholds were finally secured and enlarged. Enemy troops were forced to retreat, first from Normandy, then from large areas in France and Belgium.

After a temporary delay caused by a German counteroffensive in December 1944, the Allies drove relentlessly into Germany, crossing the Rhine River in March 1945. At that time the Soviets were pushing westward through Poland and into Germany. On April 25 American and Soviet armies met on the Elbe River in central Germany.

The final meeting of Roosevelt, Churchill, and Stalin occurred in February 1945 at Yalta in the Crimean section of Russia. Plans were made for occupying Germany and for establishing a new international peace organization, which became the United Nations. Stalin pledged that Poland and the Balkan countries—areas that the Red armies were occupying—would have free elections after the war ended.

The Germans surrendered on May 7, 1945. Two of the chief wartime leaders, Roosevelt and Hitler, died shortly before this happened. FDR suffered a fatal cerebral hemorrhage on April 12, and Vice President Harry Truman became president. Hitler committed suicide on April 30.

The United States and the British Empire now could turn their full attention to defeating Japan. Earlier in 1945, American bombers had dropped tons of incendiary bombs on Tokyo, causing massive firestorms that destroyed thousands of buildings and killed about 120,000 people. American troops had invaded the Philippines and also conquered the small island of Iwo Jima after heavy fighting. Meanwhile, British forces, commanded by Lord Louis Mountbatten, were driving the Japanese out of Burma.

American troops invaded Okinawa, a Japanese island in the Ryukyu chain, on April 1, 1945. This campaign continued for nearly three months before Americans claimed victory on June 22. Two weeks later, General Douglas MacArthur announced that the Philippines had been liberated.

The stage was now set for a possible amphibious invasion of Japan. But President Truman, fearing that such action could cause enormous casualties on both sides, instead ordered the dropping of atomic bombs on the Japanese cities of Hiroshima and Nagasaki in August. The devastating effects of these awesome bombs prompted the Japanese government to accept unconditional surrender on August 14, 1945.

The grim statistics recorded about 15 million military deaths and at least that many civilian fatalities in World War II. About 400,000 Americans had died, while the losses of Britain and its empire numbered about 500,000. France reported 620,000 victims, Japan approximately 1.25 million, and Germany more than 5 million, including many civilians. Poland had lost about 20 percent of its total population, and in Polish concentration camps, millions of Jews brought from throughout Europe were murdered in the Holocaust.

Soviet losses, military and civilian, have been estimated at between 15 and 20 million. But the Soviet Union did not reveal statistics of its total losses, perhaps because it may have intended to play an aggressive role in the postwar world and did not want other countries to know how much it had been weakened by World War II.

Great Britain and the United States were determined to overcome the Communist blockade of West Berlin that began on June 24, 1948. The allies undertook a massive airlift of supplies to the city.

SEVEN

A PERIOD OF DRAMATIC CHANGES

In 1945 the British economy was in a dreadful shape. Bombing raids had destroyed many commercial and public buildings, factories and mills, houses and churches. The war had led to a huge increase in the national debt and had caused the loss of most of Britain's export market. Consequently, the British did not have the income to pay for the imports of food that they needed and the raw materials required to operate their industries.

"Many of the conditions of war were indeed to continue until early 1950, with rationing and [price] controls enduring still longer. Yet the war itself cracked many of the conventions of British society, so that idealists could genuinely welcome the peace as heralding a new dawn."[1]

The first clear sign of this new dawn occurred on July 26, 1945, when the British voters elected members of the House of Commons. The result was a stunning victory for the Labour party over Winston Churchill's Conservative party. In the British political system, the party with the most seats in the House of Commons elects as prime minister the chief leader of that party in the House. So, less than three months after Germany and Italy had surrendered, Churchill was replaced as prime minister by Clement Attlee, the leader of the Labour party.

The British people thus chose the Labour party to guide them into the new conditions of postwar society. The changes brought about by the Labour government were swift and sweeping. Between 1946 and 1948, it removed from private ownership and placed under government control most of Britain's major industries. The Attlee government nationalized the coal industry, gas and electric production, civil aviation and railroads, telecommunications, and the Bank of England.

The National Insurance Act of 1946 greatly increased the social welfare system. The National Health Service Act of 1946—the most widely publicized social measure of the new government—provided free medical care for the British people "from the cradle to the grave."

Critics of the Labor government called its drastic changes socialistic and warned that they thwarted personal initiative, a key ingredient in the capitalist system. Defenders replied that these measures were reforms needed to cope with the nation's desperate economic conditions.

THE COLD WAR BEGINS

The alliance of the United States, Great Britain, and the Soviet Union had conquered their enemies in World War II. People everywhere hoped there would be no more wars, and a new world organization, the United Nations, had been created in 1945 to make peace permanent.

Shortly after the fighting ended, however, the alliance began coming apart at the seams. Joseph Stalin, the Communist leader of the Soviet Union, broke his pledge to allow elections in the countries of Eastern Europe and instead turned them into Soviet "puppet" states. In northern Iran, the Soviets refused to withdraw their troops, as they had promised to do.

Another serious problem was that the Soviets failed to agree with their former allies about the future of defeated Germany. The United States, Great Britain, France, and the Soviet Union had each been assigned one German zone to govern until a peace treaty could be arranged to reunite the country. But the Soviets would not permit their zone to be merged with the rest of Germany. Eventually, Germany became two countries—West Germany, which was free and democratic, and East Germany, which was Communist-controlled.

These aggressive actions by the Soviet Union marked the beginning of the so-called Cold War. They occurred at the same time that the United States and Great Britain were hastily demobilizing their armed forces. The Soviets, however, refused to disarm, and their belligerent attitude threatened the fragile peace.

Former Prime Minister Winston Churchill was deeply troubled by the Soviet Union's menacing behavior. On March 5, 1946, he expressed his fears in an important address at Westminster College in Fulton, Missouri. "From Stettin in the Baltic [Sea] to Trieste in the Adriatic [Sea], an iron curtain has descended across the Continent," he declared. The people of Eastern Europe are now "in the Soviet sphere, and are all subject, in one form or another, not only to Soviet influence, but to a very high and in some cases increasing measure of control from Moscow."

Churchill believed that the Soviets profited from the rapid demobilization of the United States and Great Britain. While he did not feel that the Communists wanted war, he said, "I am convinced that there is nothing they admire so much as strength and there is nothing for which they have less respect than for weakness, especially military weakness."

To meet the challenge prompted by Soviet aggression Churchill called for close Anglo-American cooperation. "Neither the sure prevention of war, nor the continuous rise of world organization will be gained without what I have called the fraternal association of the English-speaking peoples. This means a special relationship between the British Commonwealth and Empire and the United States."[2]

In the years that followed, the term "special relationship" often was applied to the close ties between Great Britain and the United States.

With its financial resources severely strained, the British government sought ways to lessen its overseas commitments. Two of these commitments involved Greece and Turkey; another involved Palestine.

The British had been supplying troops and financial aid to Greece, whose government was fighting a civil war against radical groups supported by Communist Bulgaria and Yugoslavia. The British also had been giving assistance to Turkey, which had come under Soviet pressure to station troops in that country and have a large voice in the control of the Dardanelles.

Early in 1947, nearly bankrupt Britain secretly informed the United States that it no longer had the finances to provide aid to Greece and Turkey. Either the Americans would have to take over this role, or both countries faced the strong possibility of falling under Communist rule.

President Truman faced this challenge quickly and decisively. Appearing before Congress on March 12, 1947, he asked for $400 million for military and economic assistance to Greece and Turkey. Congress promptly approved the appropriation that Truman requested. In the same speech, the president emphasized what came to be known as the Truman Doctrine: "I believe that it must be the policy of the United States to support free peoples who are resisting attempted subjugation by armed minorities or by outside pressure."[3]

London newspaper correspondent Henry Brandon assessed the Truman Doctrine in this way: "For Britain the plan meant the start of the reduction in her international commitments. For the United States it meant involvement in the defense of

Europe, and so was intended also to reinforce American understanding . . . of how dangerous the Russians really were to the security of the West and to Western civilization in general."[4]

BRITISH-HELD PALESTINE BECOMES INDEPENDENT ISRAEL

About one year before World War I ended, British Foreign Secretary Arthur Balfour declared his country's support for the establishment of a Jewish national homeland in Palestine. But the Arabs had lived in Palestine for centuries, and they could not be pushed aside without grave repercussions.

Palestine became a British mandate in 1920. However, since Britain was dependent on the Arab countries for oil, it took no decisive steps toward making Palestine a Jewish homeland. In fact, the British imposed strict quotas on the number of Jewish immigrants allowed to settle in their Promised Land. British naval patrols even turned back a number of steamers laden with Jewish refugees within sight of Palestine.

Still, the number of Jews in Palestine grew steadily in the 1920s and 1930s. After World War II, hundreds of thousands of European Jews who had been displaced by Hitler's cruel Holocaust migrated to Palestine, which they considered their Holy Land. By 1946 about 600,000 Jews, along with nearly 1 million Arabs, lived in Palestine.

Early in 1947, the financially exhausted British dumped their Palestine burden on the United Nations. That year a plan for partitioning Palestine between Arabs and Jews was adopted by the United Nations (UN) General Assembly, despite fierce objections from the Arab nations.

The new state of Israel was proclaimed on May 14, 1948, and President Truman immediately declared that the United States recognized its existence as an independent nation. Within hours after this new country was launched, armies from Arab countries attacked it. The Israelis fought for their homeland for many months until mediation by the United Nations provided a temporary truce in 1949.

ATTEMPTS TO CONTAIN COMMUNISM

The American help given to Greece and Turkey was the first phase of a new foreign policy known as "containment," which the United States followed for many years. The chief purpose of containment was to keep communism within its existing boundaries. It first was applied to Soviet attempts to gain control of more land and people; later, it also was applied to Communist threats by North Korea, Red China, and North Vietnam.

The economy of other European countries besides Britain had been shattered by the devastating effects of World War II. Conditions were so bad that there was a widespread fear that many Europeans might turn in desperation to communism. The postwar Communist parties in both Italy and France were attracting large numbers of new members.

In June 1947 Secretary of State George Marshall proposed a plan to revive the economies of European countries within the framework of the capitalist system. The United States would supply the funds needed to spur this recovery program, but only after the European nations had drawn up detailed plans for restoring production, pooling resources, controlling inflation, and providing careful accounting so that Americans could see how their money was spent.

Seventeen Western European nations agreed to the conditions set down by the Marshall Plan. Congress voted $13 billion to put the plan into operation. It was remarkably successful, and within a few years industrial production in the countries receiving Marshall Plan assistance had risen sharply.

Another postwar problem pertained to Berlin, which lay 110 miles (177 kilometers) inside Communist East Germany.

The city itself was divided into two sections, Communist East Berlin and non-Communist West Berlin. On June 24, 1948, the Communists suddenly closed all the highways, railroads, and water routes that ran from democratic West Germany to West Berlin. They believed that when the West Berliners no longer could get food and fuel from West Germany they would be forced to give up their freedom.

Both the United States and Great Britain were determined to prevent West Berlin from surrendering to the Communists. President Truman concluded that West Berlin could be supplied by transporting food and fuel in airplanes. If the Communists acted against the airlift, that would lead to war. American and British planes flew vast amounts of vital supplies to the people of West Berlin until, many months later, the Communists finally ended their siege of the city.

The Berlin blockade and other aggressive Communist acts convinced the European democracies that economic assistance was not enough to resist the growing perceived military threat from the Soviet Union. They decided to become allies and draw up a treaty establishing a military organization for their mutual defense. But the Europeans knew it would not be strong enough to protect them from Soviet advances unless the United States—the world's most powerful country—joined the organization.

Some Americans felt that their nation should not enter a binding commitment and contradict George Washington's long-standing warning against entangling the United States in any permanent alliances. President Truman and his advisers, however, knew that Western Europe could not stand on its feet against the Soviets without American support.

In April 1949 a treaty was negotiated that created the North Atlantic Treaty Organization (NATO). The United States, Great Britain, eight other European countries, Canada, and Iceland were the original members of NATO. The partners pledged they would develop their "individual and collective capacity to resist armed attack" and agreed "that an armed attack against any one or more of them . . . shall be considered an attack against them all."[5]

While the NATO Pact was being formulated, Lewis Douglas, the U.S. ambassador in London, observed that the British were sadly realizing that their country was no longer the superpower it once had been. "Anglo-American unity today is more firmly established than ever before in peacetime," he wrote. "But Britain has never before been in a position where her national security and economic fate are so completely dependent on and at the mercy of another country's decisions. This is a bitter pill for a country accustomed to full control of her national destiny."[6]

On June 25, 1950, the Cold War suddenly turned hot. Large numbers of Communist North Korean troops crossed the border at the 38th parallel and invaded non-Communist South Korea. The aggressors believed that with one swift, mighty stroke they could conquer their neighbors and reunite the entire Korean Peninsula under the Red flag.

Acting quickly to support South Korea, the United States took advantage of a temporary Soviet absence from the United Nations Security Council to gain that body's condemnation of North Korea as an aggressor and its approval of intervention. The Security Council recommended that UN members send troops and military equipment to repel the North Koreans.

The Truman administration decided to help defend South Korea with large-scale air, naval, and ground forces. Many other nations, including Great Britain, also responded to the UN request, but most of the fighting was done by Americans and South Koreans. General Douglas MacArthur was named commander of the UN forces.

At first, the UN troops were forced to retreat, but in September 1950 they went on the offensive and pushed the North Koreans back. When General MacArthur's armies

92

crossed the 38th parallel into North Korea and approached the Yalu River (North Korea's border with Communist China), the war suddenly took a new and ominous turn. In November 1950 about 300,000 Chinese "volunteers" poured across the Yalu and drove the UN troops back over the ground they had taken and deep into South Korea.

Strengthened by additional reserves and powerful air attacks, the UN soldiers in 1951 finally managed to force the intruders back into North Korea. Following a long stalemate, an armistice was signed in July 1953 that left Korea divided at approximately the 38th parallel.

Britain cooperated closely with the United States during the Korean War, but there was an instance when relations between the two countries were strained. On November 30, 1950, President Truman held a press conference and was asked whether the United States would consider using the atom bomb in the war. This was soon after the Chinese had intervened and begun forcing the UN troops southward. Truman responded that "there has always been consideration of its use." Then he added, "It's a matter that the military people will have to decide."[7]

British government leaders were alarmed that the use of atomic weapons could cause countless casualties and possibly expand the limited campaign in Korea into a major war against China and perhaps the Soviet Union. Prime Minister Clement Attlee hurriedly flew to Washington, D.C. There the president assured Britain's leader that the press had blown his unfortunate remarks out of proportion and that the United States would not use atom bombs without first consulting the British government.

TROUBLES IN THE MIDDLE EAST

The Suez Canal, which was owned by British and French investors, was the waterway through which passed most of

Western Europe's oil supply from the Middle East. British troops guarded the canal from 1882 until June 1956, when the last units were withdrawn in accordance with an Anglo-Egyptian treaty signed in 1954.

Egypt's president, Gamal Abdel Nasser, intended to build a dam at Aswan on the Nile River. The construction of this giant project, whose cost was estimated at $1.3 billion, would provide electric power for Egypt's industries and add about 25 percent to the country's farmland. The United States and Great Britain offered to help finance the building of the dam.

Nasser delayed his acceptance and hinted at receiving better terms from the Soviet Union, which was eager to expand its influence among the Arab countries in the Middle East. This angered the Americans and British, and the United States was further incensed when Nasser formally recognized Communist China, a nation to which the United States was still turning a cold shoulder.

Nasser's unfriendly actions caused the United States and Britain to withdraw their offer to help pay for the Aswan Dam. Furious, Nasser seized and nationalized the Suez Canal. He announced he would use part of its revenue to finance the new dam on the Nile River.

On October 29, 1956, Israel, which had recently fought back terrorist raids launched inside Egypt, attacked that country, and Israeli troops moved toward the canal. Two days later, without consulting the United States, Britain and France ordered their planes to bomb Egyptian bases, and on November 5 their paratroopers began seizing the northern portions of the canal.

The American government was shocked by this secret offensive waged by three of its closest friends. Fear that this aggression would lead to a large-scale conflict was heightened when Soviet leaders openly talked of nuclear war against Britain and France, and threatened to send Russian "volunteer" troops into Egypt.

The United Nations General Assembly was hastily convened, and the United States took the unusual step of joining with the Soviet Union to help pass a resolution condemning the military actions taken by Britain, France, and Israel. Under strong UN pressure, the invading forces were pulled out of Egypt, and a special UN police force was sent to preserve order as the British, French, and Israeli troops retreated.

Many people in Britain were appalled by the unsympathetic stand that the United States had taken during this crisis. They condemned Americans for betraying Britain at a time when it desperately needed U.S. support. Nothing that had happened in the years since World War II had so severely shaken the close Anglo-American "special relationship."

Both countries, however, wanted to heal the wound quickly. Two days after the cease-fire was proclaimed, President Dwight D. Eisenhower told the British ambassador, "Just because Britain and the U.S. had had a sharp difference over the attack on Egypt, there was no thought that we would not keep our friendship over the long term."[8]

THE BEATLES: YOUNG AMERICANS' FAVORITE BRITISH EXPORT

In the late 1950s, four talented young men from Liverpool, a seaport on the northwestern coast of England, formed a band that in 1960 became the Beatles—the world's most celebrated rock'n'roll band. It consisted of three guitar-playing singers—Paul McCartney, John Lennon, George Harrison—and drummer Pete Best, later replaced by Ringo Starr.

The group cut its first hit record, "Love Me Do," in 1962, and it was followed by the even more popular "Please Please Me" and "I Want to Hold Your Hand." As a result of these early successes, "Beatlemania" took England by storm.

When the Beatles arrived in the United States in February 1964, they already had a huge number of American fans who had been thrilled by their records. They performed on *The Ed Sullivan Show*, which played to 73 million viewers, the largest television audience to that time.

By April the Beatles held the five highest positions on the U.S. "top one hundred" singles chart, and by the end of the year they had an incredible twenty-nine hits on the chart. In 1964 they also made the film *A Hard Day's Night*.

The Beatles' ability to relate in a personal way to audiences, especially teenagers, was phenomenal. The appeal of this group sprang from the songs they composed and performed expertly, their irrepressible spirit and buoyant charm, and, of course, their distinctive hairstyle.

After a final concert in San Francisco in 1966, the Beatles were exhausted from touring and limited their work to making records until they disbanded in 1970. Efforts to bring them back together ended when Lennon was tragically murdered in 1980.

Beginning with the 1964 arrival of the Beatles in America, this period of popular music was called the "British Invasion" because various vocal groups from England toured and made hit records in the United States. Other popular British groups of the mid-1960s were the Rolling Stones, the Who, and Herman's Hermits.

GREAT BRITAIN AND THE VIETNAM WAR

During the presidential administrations of Dwight D. Eisenhower and John F. Kennedy, the United States sent financial aid and a limited number of military advisers to non-Communist South Vietnam to help defend that country against a takeover by Communist North Vietnam. But after Lyndon B. Johnson became president in November 1963, American participation in the war was greatly increased. By the end of 1965, Johnson had sent 160,000 U.S. troops to fight against the North Vietnamese and the Vietcong, their Communist al-

96

lies in South Vietnam. By 1968 American armed forces in Vietnam exceeded half a million.

The American president hoped that Britain would send at least a token military force to Vietnam. He told British Prime Minister Harold Wilson that even a small contingent of Britons would provide a strong psychological boost for the American cause. "A platoon of bagpipers would be sufficient," Johnson declared. "It was the British flag that was wanted."[9]

Wilson, however, had to govern with a very small majority in a Parliament that included many opponents of the Vietnam War, and public opinion was in such a mood that he dared not send British troops to the Vietnamese battlefields. England witnessed some violent demonstrations against the war. On October 27, 1968, a huge crowd of antiwar young people fought with mounted police in London and broke the windows of the American Embassy.

President Johnson never forgave the British for failing to contribute to a war that the United States ultimately lost. In his memoirs, he bitterly wrote, "I have no doubt . . . that the British government's general approach to the war and to finding a peaceful solution would have been considerably different if a brigade of Her Majesty's forces had been stationed . . . in Vietnam."[10]

97

Tourism between Great Britain and the United States helps
to unify their relationship and to support the economies of both
countries. In this photo, tourists enjoy a parade of the
Life Guards at Whitehall, London.

EIGHT

ANGLO-AMERICAN RELATIONS IN RECENT YEARS

In 1979 Margaret Thatcher became the first woman prime minister of Great Britain. She held that office for eleven years—longer than any other prime minister since Lord Liverpool, who had served from 1812 to 1827.

As the leader of the Conservative party, Thatcher—often called the "Iron Lady"—brought about major changes in the British economy. She reined in the labor unions, whose powers had grown unwieldy. The Thatcher government "privatized" (returned to private ownership) many of the industries and businesses that had been nationalized shortly after World War II. British Airways and British Steel were two examples of large corporations that had failed to prosper under government control and became profitable after they were privatized. In an attempt to stimulate the economy by fostering private initiative, the Thatcher administration waged an effective campaign to reduce inflation, cut income taxes, and lessen the restrictions imposed on businesses by the government. However, during the world recession of the early 1980s, unemployment in Britain more than tripled between 1979 and 1983.

One of Thatcher's strongest admirers was Ronald Reagan, who became president about eighteen months after she had assumed the highest position in the British government. He shared Thatcher's conservative philosophy. During President Reagan's administration, taxes and inflation in the United States were lowered, businesses were freed from many government regulations, and wider market opportunities for free enterprise were encouraged. At the same time, however, the United States had the largest budget deficit in its history.

Thatcher and Reagan turned their warm friendship into a powerful foreign policy partnership. She applauded Reagan's huge buildup of American armaments, and both of them took a hard-line stance in dealings with the Soviet Union.

In the final month of Reagan's second term, Thatcher praised the president, declaring ". . . he has achieved the most difficult of all political tasks: changing attitudes and perceptions about what is possible. From the strong fortress of his convictions, he set out to enlarge freedom the world over at a time when freedom was in retreat—and he succeeded."[1]

Margaret Thatcher stepped down as prime minister in 1990 and was succeeded by John Major, another leader of the Conservative party.

WAR IN THE FALKLAND ISLANDS

The Falkland Islands (also called the Malvinas) in the South Atlantic Ocean are British colonies. They include two large islands and many smaller ones, lying 300 miles (483 kilometers) east of the Straits of Magellan. Although there are only about 2,300 settlers on the islands today, they are mainly of British descent and content to live under the British flag.

For many decades Argentina claimed ownership of these islands that are near its coast. After several years of fruitless negotiations between Argentina and Britain, Argentine military forces invaded the Falkland Islands on April 2, 1982. They easily forced the surrender of a small contingent of British marines.

Prime Minister Margaret Thatcher decided to prove that Britain still had enough military muscle to defend the remote islands and punish armed aggression. She ordered a sizable task force, including many aircraft, ships, and two aircraft carriers, be sent to the South Atlantic. Large passenger ships, such as the *Queen Elizabeth II*, were packed with soldiers, military equipment, and supplies.

While the conflict was brewing, Americans were slow to take sides between two friends of the United States and hoped a settlement could be arranged. Secretary of State Alexander Haig undertook rigorous shuttle diplomacy between London and Buenos Aires in an unsuccessful attempt to bring both nations to the peace table.

After the British military forces began to move against the islands' Argentine invaders, the United States finally took a firm stand in favor of Britain. On April 30, President Ronald Reagan declared that "the aggression was on the part of Argentina in this dispute . . . and I think the principle that all of us must abide by is, armed aggression of that kind must not be allowed to succeed."[2]

The United States helped the British cause in various ways. It gave Britain valuable secret military intelligence from signals that had been intercepted. It also provided about two hundred air to air missiles, staging facilities, ammunition, aircraft fuel, and an array of spare parts.

The Argentines were overwhelmed by the superior British forces and surrendered on June 14, 1982. British losses in the conflict totaled 255 military deaths and six ships. But Britons felt proud of their military personnel for putting down aggressors on a far-distant shore.

BRITAIN'S SHRINKING EMPIRE

One of the most important chapters in the history of Great Britain since World War II deals with the breakup of the British Empire.

101

For many years India's great Hindu leader, Mohandas Gandhi, worked to free his homeland from British rule. Muslim leaders, however, demanded that parts of India become a separate Muslim country. Despite Gandhi's fervent plea for unity, in 1947 two independent nations, Hindu India and Muslim Pakistan, were carved out of South Asia. Two other Asian lands, Burma and Ceylon (now Sri Lanka), achieved independence in 1948.

After centuries of almost ceaseless conflict between Catholic Ireland and Protestant England, the Irish Free State that had been established as a British dominion in 1921 became a totally independent republic in 1949. Protestant Ulster, which occupies the northeastern portion of the island of Ireland, remained a part of Great Britain.

The Union of South Africa had become a self-governing British dominion in 1910. It left the Commonwealth in 1961 and became an independent republic. For many years South Africa was the scene of constant turmoil between the small white minority and the large black majority. The governing white population maintained a system of rigid racial segregation known as apartheid.

Many nations expressed opposition to apartheid by banning trade with South Africa and not allowing its athletes to compete in international sports events. Gradually, the South African government repealed its apartheid laws. The country held its first elections open to blacks in 1994. Nelson Mandela, who had been imprisoned for nearly twenty-six years because he led the fight against racial discrimination, became South Africa's first black president.

Most of the other British possessions in both Africa and Asia gained their independence in the 1950s and 1960s. In the Western Hemisphere, Jamaica became a self-ruling member of the British Commonwealth in 1962, and freedom was won the same year by Trinidad and Tobago. Barbados achieved Commonwealth status in 1966 and the Bahamas in 1973. British Guiana in South America became the independent nation of Guyana in 1966. Belize (formerly British Honduras) was Britain's last colony on the American mainland, and it became a Commonwealth member in 1981.

Following the first Opium War that ended in 1842, victorious Britain took Hong Kong from China. Over a period of many years when it had a capitalist system, Hong Kong prospered as a center of trade and industry. But when China became a Communist country shortly after World War II, it demanded that Britain return Hong Kong. Lengthy negotiations ensued, and finally in 1984 Britain agreed to hand over Hong Kong to China in 1997, providing China promised to let it keep its capitalist system for fifty years after that date. When Hong Kong was transferred to Communist China in 1997, the British government felt it had lost the jewel of its Crown colonies.

The most important parts of the small British Empire today are Gibraltar, the Falkland Islands, Bermuda, the British Virgin Islands, Montserrat, the Cayman Islands, and the Pitcairn Islands Group.

NEW TRADE PATTERNS AND CULTURAL EXCHANGES

While the British Empire was shrinking, an important economic development was occurring in Western Europe. In 1957 France, West Germany, Italy, the Netherlands, Belgium, and Luxembourg formed the European Economic Community (EEC), popularly known as the European Common Market. Even though the United States prodded Britain to join this union, at first the British held back. They said they preferred to concentrate on seeking stronger economic ties with the Commonwealth countries and the United States.

The European Common Market became remarkably successful as barriers to trade among the member nations were gradually abolished. Manufactured goods and raw materials flowed tariff-free from country to country, and trade among the EEC members soon tripled.

103

By 1963 both West Germany and France had stronger economies than Britain's, and leaders of the British government decided the time had come to seek membership in the EEC. But President Charles de Gaulle of France vetoed Britain's application in 1963 and again in 1967. De Gaulle did not want Britain to rival France's leadership of the Common Market. Also, "De Gaulle remained convinced that Britain would seek to maintain its special relationship with the Americans and be only a half-hearted member of the EEC."[3]

After de Gaulle stepped down from office, Great Britain entered the EEC in 1973. The EEC in 1993 merged with the European Coal and Steel Community and the European Atomic Energy Commission to become the European Union (EU). Today, there are fifteen member nations in the EU. Its population is larger than that of the United States, and it has 18.6 percent of world trade compared with 16.6 percent for the United States.

The European Monetary Union (EMU), a branch of the EU, is introducing a common currency called the euro for the area known as "Euroland." Eleven of its members already have agreed to use this currency. Jurgen Stark, a high official in the German Financial Ministry, said that this EMU project "will have no parallel in history."[4] Four EU nations—Britain, Sweden, Denmark, and Greece—have, for the time being, bypassed the first euro wave, but may adopt the new currency later.

The gradual introduction of the common European currency began in early 1999, and it affected mainly bankers, stockbrokers, and the international business community. Then, in 2002, after the new money has been minted and distributed, Europeans who have accepted this new monetary system will relinquish their familiar francs, marks, liras, and other national monies and begin using the same euros and bank notes.

Traditionally, the British and Americans have been very active trading partners, but since Britain joined the European

Common Market its volume of trade with the United States has sharply declined. In 1996 the United States accounted for only 12 percent of Britain's imports and 11 percent of its exports. In the same year, the EU accounted for 52 percent of Britain's imports and 57 percent of its exports.

Britain and the United States, however, continue to share much technical and sensitive information, especially in defense matters. Also, in the late 1990s, some large British and American corporations that are within the same industry proposed some mergers or alliances and carried out others. American Airlines and British Airways have planned an alliance. The two carriers currently control 60 percent of the transatlantic market between Britain and the United States, and once allied, they would have 90 percent of the market on seventeen routes. British Telecom and American Telephone and Telegraph Company are seeking approval by the European Union and the United States government to form an alliance that would serve the global communication needs of multinational companies. In the world's largest industrial merger, energy giants British Petroleum and Amoco Corporation of Chicago became a single corporation. This merger reshapes the business of searching for oil and natural gas and turning those natural resources into more products that benefit consumers.

One of Britain's most lucrative industries is tourism, and each year it draws to the British Isles about 15 million visitors, including a large number of Americans. Tourists enjoy spending time in the green rolling hills of Ireland and England's lake district, the craggy Scottish Highlands, and the bleak, windswept moors of southern England.

There are scores of fascinating attractions in Britain, including three spectacular ones launched in the 1990s. The English Channel Tunnel, a marvel of modern engineering that was opened in 1994, links the coasts of France and England over a distance of about 31 miles (50 kilometers). It provides underwater transportation for cars and trains. William

Shakespeare's famous Globe Theatre was carefully reconstructed in London on the banks of the Thames River and celebrated its opening season in 1997.

The third special project is underway at Greenwich, a town a short distance east of London. Greenwich lies on the meridian line marking zero degrees of longitude, from which time zones are figured. Technically, the next millennium (period of 1,000 years) that begins at the start of the twenty-first century will first occur at Greenwich. To celebrate this event, the British are constructing there a huge billion-dollar Millennium Dome, twice the size of England's largest soccer stadium.

Cultural exchanges between Britain and the United States are plentiful. British students often attend American colleges, and Americans frequently study at such distinguished British universities as Oxford, Cambridge, and East Anglia in Norwich, England. Each year a few of the highest qualified college graduates in the British Empire and the United States are selected as Rhodes scholars. These scholarships, established by Cecil Rhodes, who made a fortune in diamond mining, are for postgraduate studies at Oxford University.

There is a ceaseless transatlantic exchange of books, plays, motion pictures, television programs, and both popular and classical musical productions. For example, the musical shows by Briton Andrew Lloyd Weber have been warmly received in the United States, and the plays by American Neil Simon have attracted large British audiences.

COOPERATION CONTINUES IN FOREIGN AFFAIRS

On August 2, 1990, Saddam Hussein, the dictator of Iraq, sent a large army and many tanks into the small but oil-rich nation of Kuwait. Within twelve hours, all of defenseless Kuwait was occupied. Other Iraqi troops were poised on the border of Saudi Arabia—the largest oil producer in the Middle East— and an anxious world wondered whether they would invade that country, which supplies much of the oil needed for the industrial economy of many nations.

The United Nations quickly responded by imposing stringent economic sanctions on Iraq, cutting off its trade with other nations. "Economic sanctions can be very, very effective, if fully enforced," declared President George Bush in the early days of the crisis.[5] It was widely believed that Saddam would withdraw his armed forces from Kuwait once he realized that the international quarantine would shut off Iraq's imports and exports.

When Saddam refused to back down, American troops, warplanes, and naval ships began moving to Saudi Arabia. President Bush worked tirelessly to forge a coalition of nations opposed to Iraq's aggression. Some Arab countries joined the anti-Iraq coalition and accepted Israel as an ally, thus bringing together on the same side Muslims and Jews who had long been enemies. Among the European nations, the two that pledged the most help were Great Britain and France.

By a unanimous vote on November 29, 1990, the United Nations Security Council authorized UN members "to use all necessary means" to bring about an immediate and unconditional Iraqi withdrawal from Kuwait. The resolution gave Iraq until January 15, 1991, to comply; failure to do so would allow the coalition to move militarily against the invaders.

Saddam Hussein refused to recall his troops from Kuwait, and the day after the deadline passed, the United States and its allies went to war. The conflict was extremely one-sided and lasted only forty-three days. After less than six weeks of intensively bombing Iraqi targets, a massive ground assault was launched that continued for four days. The overpowered Iraqi troops showed little resistance, and Saddam accepted a cease-fire. As part of the cease-fire agreement, Iraq promised to destroy all biological and chemical weapons and allow UN observers to inspect the sites where these weapons had been made and stored.

Britain's contribution to the victory in the Persian Gulf War had been second only to that of the United States. The British had sent into the conflict thousands of trained troops, plus aircraft, ships, and military equipment. British and American armed services worked smoothly together under the command of U.S. General Norman Schwarzkopf.

The United States and Great Britain again joined together in another area of turbulence and bloodshed, Bosnia and Herzegovina. In the early 1990s, savage fighting occurred among the small countries that previously had been parts of Yugoslavia. Following a 1995 agreement signed by the leaders of Bosnia, Croatia, and Serbia, about 60,000 NATO troops, including many from the United States and Great Britain, moved into this troubled region to perform a peacekeeping mission.

Despite the defeat of Iraq in 1991, Saddam Hussein continued to be a source of concern to the international community. In 1997 and 1998, President Bill Clinton sent standby American military forces to the Persian Gulf near Iraq to force Saddam to comply with his pledge to permit United Nations observers to inspect the sites of biological and chemical weapons. Britain was the only European country to support this American display of military strength.

In December 1998 Saddam ordered the UN observers expelled from his country. This prompted the United States and Great Britain to launch a joint four-day bombing and missile attack on strategic targets in Iraq.

THE TRANSATLANTIC FRIENDSHIP PERSISTS

On May 1, 1997, British voters went to the polls and gave the Labour party a stunning victory over the Conservative party that had ruled the nation for eighteen years. Labour candidates won 419 seats in the House of Commons to 165 for the Conservatives; smaller parties acquired a total of 76 seats.

Tony Blair, the leader of the Labour party since 1994, became the new prime minister.

Bill Clinton was elected president in 1992 and reelected in 1996. His reputation was severely tarnished in 1998 when the House of Representatives impeached him on charges of committing perjury and obstructing justice. But the Senate failed to convict him, so Clinton was not removed from office.

Blair and Clinton have many similarities. Both attended Oxford University (Blair as an undergraduate, Clinton as a graduate student). As young men, Clinton enjoyed playing the saxophone; Blair strummed a bass guitar and was the lead singer in a rock band called the Ugly Rumours. Also, both have lawyer wives. Both men have had lengthy careers in government service, Clinton as Arkansas governor for ten years, Blair as a member of Parliament since 1983. Blair became prime minister at the age of forty-three; Clinton was forty-six when he became president.

The similarities between Clinton and Blair are also expressed in their political views. The American president considers himself a *new* Democrat—a political moderate who opposes the huge government expenditures made by earlier Democratic administrations. In his second term as president, working with a Republican-dominated Congress, he was able to help balance the budget for the first time in many years, reform the welfare system, which had grown unwieldy, and promote better educational opportunities for America's young people.

Blair declares that he also is a moderate who leads a *new* Labour party, one no longer dominated by trade unions and stripped of the socialist ideas that had prevailed in previous Labour administrations. He pledges that he will not increase overall government spending, restore union power, or nationalize again the industries that had been privatized by Conservative prime ministers Margaret Thatcher and John Major.

Blair, however, believes that the government does have a

role to play in helping people and assuring social justice. In his first year in office, he poured an additional $3.3 billion into the National Health Service, which provides free medical care for all Britons, and he promised to reduce the length of time patients have to wait for nonemergency medical procedures.

"He is spending $4.33 billion on a welfare-to-work training program for young unemployed [people]. The program is not unlike Bill Clinton's welfare-reform plan and assures that the best thing for the poor and disadvantaged is education, so that they can pull themselves up by their bootstraps."[6]

An impressive example of the teamwork demonstrated by Blair and Clinton was the way they worked together in trying to find a solution to the terrible strife in Northern Ireland. For thirty years this region has been the scene of intermittent fighting between its Protestant majority and its Catholic minority, supported by the Irish Republican Army (IRA). Terrorist shootings and bombings have taken more than three thousand lives. The Protestants insisted that Northern Ireland remain part of Great Britain; the Catholics wanted it united with the Irish Republic.

In 1996 the governments of Britain and Ireland, along with the chief leaders of the warring factions in Northern Ireland, began lengthy discussions about bringing peace to this troubled region. Heading the talks was a neutral American—George Mitchell, the capable former senator from Maine. He received major assistance from President Clinton, who frequently phoned Blair and the other negotiators, urging them to lay aside long-standing differences in the quest for an agreement acceptable to both sides.

In April 1998 after twenty-two months of intense negotiations, a settlement was reached that called for replacing terrorism with democracy and letting the people of Northern Ireland decide their own ultimate fate. The peace agreement established a new 108-member assembly to govern Northern

Ireland, replacing direct rule from London. The assembly is structured to guarantee fair representation of the Catholic minority. The agreement also set up a political body called the North/South Ministerial Council with representatives of both Northern Ireland and the Republic of Ireland. It will oversee concerns that affect all of Ireland, such as agriculture, trade, and tourism.

Whether the peace settlement in Northern Ireland will be permanent or only temporary cannot be told at this time. But Prime Minister Blair is grateful for the role played by the United States in helping to bring about the agreement.

Although it can be argued that today the Anglo-American ties are not as binding as they were in World War II when Britain's very survival was at stake, the special relationship between the United States and Great Britain is still alive and thriving.

CHRONOLOGY

1607 First permanent English settlement at Jamestown, Virginia

1619 First African blacks are brought to Jamestown

1707 England and Scotland unite to create Great Britain

1756–1763 Seven Years' War between Britain and France

1765 Stamp Act passed; repealed in 1766

1773 Boston Tea Party leads to Intolerable Acts

1774 First Continental Congress convenes

1775 Second Continental Congress meets

1775–1783 American Revolutionary War

1776 Declaration of Independence is adopted

1778 French-American alliance is formed

1789 United States government begins

1794 Jay's Treaty stalls second war with Britain

1807 Embargo Act ends foreign trade

1812–1815	War of 1812
1817	Rush–Bagot Pact demilitarizes Great Lakes
1823	United States proclaims Monroe Doctrine
1842	Webster–Ashburton Treaty settles Maine-New Brunswick border
1846	Oregon territory is divided at 49th parallel
1850	Clayton–Bulwer Treaty: Central American canal will be joint Anglo–U.S. project
1861–1865	United States Civil War
1895	Venezuela–British Guiana controversy
1901	Hay–Pauncefote Treaty: U.S. alone will build Central American canal
1914	World War I begins
1917	United States enters World War I
1918	Central Powers are defeated
1921–1922	Naval disarmament by major powers
1935–1937	Congress passes neutrality acts
1938	Munich Conference appeases Hitler
1939	Nazis invade Poland to start World War II
1940	Winston Churchill becomes British prime minister
1940	U.S. destroyers traded for British bases
1941	Congress approves lend-lease policy
1941	United States enters World War II
1945	United Nations is formed
1945	Atomic bombs dropped on Japanese cities
1945	World War II ends as Japan surrenders
1946	Churchill calls for U.S.–British opposition to Soviet aggression

1947	U.S. replaces Britain as source of aid to Greece and Turkey
1947	Marshall Plan helps European economies
1948	United States recognizes state of Israel
1948–1949	Berlin blockade
1949	NATO is created
1950–1953	Korean War
1956	United States opposes attack on Suez Canal by Britain, France, and Israel
1968	Britons demonstrate against Vietnam War
1973	Britain joins European Common Market
1979	Margaret Thatcher becomes British prime minister
1982	British-Argentine war in Falkland Islands
1990	John Major becomes British prime minister
1991	Persian Gulf War against Iraq
1994	English Channel Tunnel opens
1995–1998	NATO peacekeepers stationed in Bosnia
1997	Tony Blair becomes British prime minister
1997–1998	Britain backs U.S. sending standby military forces to Iraq
1998	United States helps negotiators reach accord in Northern Ireland
1998	United States and Britain launch four-day bombing and missile attack on strategic targets in Iraq

SOURCE NOTES

CHAPTER ONE
1. F.E. Halliday, *A Concise History of England from Stonehenge to the Atomic Age* (New York: Thames and Hudson, 1980), p. 31.

CHAPTER TWO
1. Paul Langford, "The Eighteenth Century: The Politics of Protest," in *The Oxford History of Britain*, Kenneth 0. Morgan, ed. (Oxford, UK: Oxford University Press, 1993), p. 450.
2. Elinor Goettel, *America's Wars—Why?* (Evanston, IL: McDougal, Littell, 1974), p. 24.
3. Page Smith, *A New Age Now Begins* (New York: McGraw-Hill, 1976), p. 257.
4. Pauline Maier, *American Scripture: Making the Declaration of Independence* (New York: Knopf, 1997), p. 3.
5. Goettel, *America's Wars*, p. 24.
6. Maier, *American Scripture*, p. 23.
7. Thomas Fleming, *Liberty! The American Revolution* (New York: Viking, 1997), p. 338.

CHAPTER THREE
1. Lawrence James, *The Rise and Fall of the British Empire* (New York: St. Martin's Press, 1994), p. 119.

2. Eugene P. Link, *Democratic-Republican Societies, 1790–1800* (New York: Columbia University Press, 1942), p. 46.
3. Richard J. Barnet, *The Rockets' Red Glare: When America Goes to War* (New York: Simon and Schuster, 1990), p. 25.
4. Ernest Sutherland Bates, *The Story of Congress: 1789–1935* (New York: Harper, 1936), p. 29.

CHAPTER FOUR
1. Birdsall S. Viault, *English History* (New York: McGraw-Hill, 1992), p. 223.
2. Bradford Perkins, *The Creation of a Republican Empire, 1776–1865* (New York: Cambridge University Press, 1995), p. 163.
3. Stanley Meisler, "Lots of Gems, No Diamond," *Los Angeles Times*, February 4, 1996, Calendar, p. 4.
4. Ibid.
5. Paul F. Boller, Jr., *Presidential Campaigns* (New York: Oxford University Press, 1984), p. 79.
6. David M. Pletcher, "James K. Polk," in *The Presidents: A Reference History,* Henry Graff, ed. (New York: Macmillan, 1997), pp. 160–161.
7. Ibid., p. 161.
8. Thomas A. Bailey, *A Diplomatic History of the American People* (Englewood Cliffs, NJ: Prentice-Hall, 1980), p. 227.

CHAPTER FIVE
1. William R. Brock, *Conflict and Transformation: The United States, 1844–1877* (New York: Penguin Books, 1973), p. 173.
2. Perkins, *The Creation of a Republican Empire*, p. 224.
3. Ibid., p. 226.
4. Ibid., p. 228.
5. Bill Kelly, "P.T. Barnum's Biggest Star," *American History*, February, 1998, p. 39.
6. Irving Wallace, *The Fabulous Showman: The Life and Times of P.T. Barnum* (New York: Knopf, 1959), p. 244.
7. Charles S. Campbell, *From Revolution to Rapprochement: The United States and Great Britain, 1783–1900* (New York: John Wiley, 1974), p. 183.
8. Quoted in Walter LaFeber, *The American Age: United States*

Foreign Policy at Home and Abroad Since 1750 (New York: Norton, 1989), p. 174.

9. David Dimbleby and David Reynolds, *An Ocean Apart: The Relationship Between Britain and America in the Twentieth Century* (New York: Random House, 1988), pp. 30-31.

10. Meirion and Susie Harries, *The Last Days of Innocence: America at War, 1917–1918* (New York: Random House, 1997), p. 40.

CHAPTER SIX

1. R.R. Palmer and Joel Cotton, *A History of the Modern World* (New York: Knopf, 1961), p. 795.

2. Ibid., p. 817.

3. Robin Renwick, *Fighting with Allies: America and Britain in Peace and at War* (New York: Times Books, 1996) p. 24.

4. Akira Iriye, *The Globalizing of America, 1913–1945* (New York: Cambridge University Press, 1995), p. 165.

5. Warren F. Kimball, ed., *Churchill and Roosevelt: The Complete Correspondence* (Princeton, NJ: Princeton University Press, 1984), vol. 1, p. 57.

6. Richard M. Ketchum, *The Borrowed Years, 1938–1941: America on the Way to War* (New York: Random House, 1989), p. 478.

7. Ibid., p. 479.

8. Quoted in LaFeber, *The American Age*, p. 382.

9. Kimball, *Churchill and Roosevelt*, p. 283.

10. Kenneth 0. Morgan, *The People's Peace: British History, 1945–1990* (Oxford, UK: Oxford University Press, 1992), p. 12.

11 Robert Rhodes James, ed., *Winston S. Churchill: His Complete Speeches, 1897-1963*, (New York. Chelsea House, 1984), vol 6, p. 6695.

CHAPTER SEVEN

1. Arthur Marwick, *British Society Since 1945* (New York: Penguin Books, 1996), p. 18.

2. Robin Renwick, *Fighting with Allies: America and Britain in Peace and at War* (New York: Times Books, 1996), pp. 128–129.

3. Birdsall S. Viault, *English History* (New York: McGraw-Hill, 1992), p. 423.
4. Henry Brandon, *Special Relationships: A Foreign Correspondent's Memoirs from Roosevelt to Reagan* (New York: Atheneum, 1988), pp. 36-37.
5. Walter LaFeber, *The American Age: United States Foreign Policy at Home and Abroad Since 1750* (New York: Norton, 1989), p. 467.
6. *Foreign Relations of the United States* (Washington, D.C.: Department of State, U.S. Government Printing Office, 1948), vol. 3, p. 1113.
7. *The Public Papers of the Presidents: Harry S. Truman, 1950* (Washington, D.C.: U.S. Government Printing Office, 1965), p. 727.
8. Renwick, *Fighting with Allies*, p. 225.
9. Ibid., p, 282.
10. Lyndon B. Johnson, *The Vantage Point: Perspectives of the Presidency, 1963–1969.* (New York: Holt, Rinehart and Winston, 1971), p. 255.

CHAPTER EIGHT
1. Quoted in Lou Cannon, *President Reagan: The Role of a Lifetime* (New York: Simon and Schuster, 1991), p. 465.
2. Quoted in David Dimbleby and David Reynolds, *An Ocean Apart: The Relationship Between Britain and America in the Twentieth Century* (New York: Random House, 1988), p. 334.
3. Henry Brandon, *Special Relationships: A Foreign Correspondent's Memoirs from Roosevelt to Reagan* (New York, Atheneum, 1988), p. 164.
4. Michael Hirsh, "Here's Why You Need to Know about the Euro," *Newsweek*, May 4, 1998, p. 40.
5. Jean Edward Smith, *George Bush's War* (New York: Holt, 1992), p. 100.
6. Barry Hillenbrand, "King of the World," *Time*, May 8, 1998, p. 61.

FURTHER READING

Barnet, Richard J. *The Rockets' Red Glare: When America Goes to War.* New York: Simon and Schuster, 1990.

Blumenthal, Shirley, and Jerome S. Ozer. *Coming to America: Immigrants from the British Isles.* New York: Delacorte, 1980.

Bradley, John. *Churchill and the British.* Danbury, CT: Franklin Watts, 1990.

Brandon, Henry. *Special Relationships: A Foreign Correspondent's Memoirs from Roosevelt to Reagan.* New York: Atheneum, 1988.

Carter, Alden R. *The War of 1812: Second Fight for Independence.* Danbury, CT: Franklin Watts, 1990.

Collier, Basil. *The Lion and the Eagle: British and Anglo-American Strategy, 1900–1950.* New York: Putnam, 1972.

Cornelius, James M. *The English Americans.* New York: Chelsea House, 1990.

Cross, Robin. *Roosevelt and the Americans at War.* Danbury, CT: Franklin Watts, 1990.

Dimbleby, David, and David Reynolds. *An Ocean Apart: The Relationship Between Britain and America in the Twentieth Century.* New York: Random House, 1988.

Fleming, Thomas. *Liberty! The American Revolution.* New York: Viking, 1997.

121

Foster, Leila M. *Margaret Thatcher, First Woman Prime Minister of Great Britain*. Danbury, CT: Children's Press, 1990.

Furer, Howard B. *The British in America, 1578–1970*. Dobbs Ferry, NY: Oceana Publications, 1972.

Grant, Neil. *United Kingdom*. Englewood Cliffs, NJ: Silver Burdett, 1988.

Halliday, F.E. *A Concise History of England from Stonehenge to the Atomic Age*. New York: Thames and Hudson, 1980.

Heater, Derek. *The Cold War*. Danbury, CT: Franklin Watts, 1989.

James, Lawrence. *The Rise and Fall of the British Empire*. New York: St. Martin's Press, 1994.

Judd, Denis. *Empire: The British Imperial Experience from 1765 to the Present*. New York: Basic Books, 1996.

LaFeber, Walter. *The American Age: United States Foreign Policy at Home and Abroad Since 1750*. New York: Norton, 1989.

Laqueur, Walter. *Europe in Our Time: A History, 1945–1992*. New York: Penguin Books, 1992.

Louis, William Roger, and Hedley Bull, eds. *The "Special Relationship": Anglo-American Relations Since 1945*. New York: Oxford University Press, 1986.

Middlekauff, Robert. *The Glorious Cause: The American Revolution, 1763-1789*. New York: Oxford University Press, 1982.

Morgan, Kenneth O., ed. *The Oxford History of Britain*. Oxford, UK: Oxford University Press, 1993.

———. *The People's Peace: British History, 1945–1990*. Oxford, UK: Oxford University Press, 1992.

Reische, Diana. *Founding the American Colonies*. Danbury, CT: Franklin Watts, 1990.

Renwick, Robin. *Fighting with Allies: America and Britain in Peace and at War*. New York: Times Books, 1996.

Viault, Birdsall S. *English History*. New York: McGraw-Hill, 1992.

INDEX

Page numbers in *italics* refer to illustrations.

ABOUT THE AUTHOR

Edmund Lindop is both a writer and a teacher. He is the recipient of a presidential commendation for "conveying the meaning of ideas and the nobility of ideals" to young people.

Great Britain and the United States is Edmund Lindop's thirty-ninth nonfiction book for youngsters. During the 1990s, he has written seven other books for Twenty-First Century Books: *Panama and the United States*, *Political Parties* in the Inside Government series, and five books in the Presidents Who Dared series.

His other recent books are *The Changing Supreme Court*, *Presidents Versus Congress*, *Assassinations That Shook America*, and *Presidents by Accident*. He contributed twenty-five articles to the encyclopedic *Young Reader's Companion to American History*.

For thirty-eight years Lindop taught history and government classes at the middle-school and high-school levels in Los Angeles, where he lives with his wife, Esther. He trained new social studies teachers at three universities.

Lindop's paternal family roots were planted in Manchester, England. He has visited the land of his ancestors several times, and these trips were educationally rewarding and exhilarating experiences.